UNSHAKABLE

SWAGGER

The Man's Guide to Being Confident Any Time,

Any Place...Period.

BYRON VAN PELT

ISBN: 978-0-615-92502-8

Printed in the USA by Ingram Spark.

Cover design: Pixel Dizajn Studio
(http://www.pixeldizajn.com/en)

Typeset in Georgia and Garamond

This book is dedicated to my incredible wife, Bethany. Thanks for your never-ending support. I love you, Bronco.

TABLE OF CONTENTS

INTRODUCTION

Unshakable Swagger has been designed to take you through a deeper approach to building self-confidence and social influence. It was created to teach you exactly how to elevate your confidence in a multitude of situations in life in a way that gives you complete access to shifting and correcting what you see fit. It is my goal to give you powerful techniques for overcoming any shyness, anxiety, and insecurities you have around others – whether you're in front of one person or one thousand.

I'm about to download a TON of new information into your brain. This is a deep book – there's a lot more here than you'd expect given the subject matter. There is a ton to uncover and if you pay attention, you can start taking immediate steps to transforming your life.

It's going to take more than just throwing on a new outfit, getting a haircut, and gobbling down ten quick feel-good tips to reach a higher level of confidence. I have endeavored to share with you all that I know about this topic, but you must be willing to meet me half way. Many of the strategies will only work if you extend yourself outside of your comfort zone, so be open to actively trying these ideas out for yourself.

Here is how I suggest you digest the material:

1. Read it once quickly – in a week or less if you can.

2. Then take your time with the second reading – write down notes and ideas that come to you. The more you dialogue with the pages, the more you will understand them.

3. As you start implementing these ideas into your life, refer back to the book to jog your memory and inspire you to

try new actions and techniques. Pay close attention to areas you may not fully grasp or understand, especially any sections where your mind feels hesitant to try out.

It's taken me a long time to get all of this down onto paper. I've spent years mixing and crafting this recipe so that you can implement all of the information in layers. Don't assume after reading this book once you have completely mastered all of the material.

You need to approach this knowledge like learning to ride a bike. At first, you go through a good bit of trial and error, maybe even falling off the bike a few times and getting scraped up. Training your body and mind to behave in new ways will feel "weird" and "unnatural" – understand that this is perfectly normal. Eventually you will be riding the bike with ease, pulling stunts and riding with no hands if you desire.

So keep at it, and know that the more you practice, the more you will see widespread changes in your life.

Let's get to work…

PART ONE:
THE FOUNDATION

In order to achieve great things,
we must prepare for them.

1

WHAT IS UNSHAKABLE SWAGGER?

"Before you can do something, you must first be something." – Goethe

I used to be a weak, vulnerable shell of a man.

At an earlier time in my life, I was extremely frustrated with the lack of appreciation I seemed to be getting from others and more importantly, the total lack of respect I had for myself. I had racked up a healthy collection of lonely nights, embarrassing mistakes, and social rejection. In school I was bullied and teased for my lack of confidence and "goofy" personality. In the dating world, I was ignored and rejected by countless women. In sales, I was told on a seemingly daily basis that I needed to get another line of work. One guy even told me I sucked so much that I'd be better off selling women's shoes. Several times I questioned the point of trying to find happiness since I failed at everything I attempted.

One of the most painful nights I can remember had me leaving my cell phone and wallet at home and just driving out to the beach where I lived. I sat there in the sand for what seemed like the entire night simply watching the waves crash. I was pissed off, saddened, and confused, mumbling, "What do I have to do?" over and over again like a mantra.

I knew there had to be a way to get what I wanted from life. I knew that some people had what I desired and that somewhere along the way I had completely failed at discovering the formula to acquiring it. That night, I decided I wasn't going to leave until I received an answer to my question. After hours of repeating, "What do I have to do?" something suddenly clicked inside. I realized that I was looking in the wrong direction for my solution. I was actually asking the wrong question; the answer wasn't to be found in what I needed to *do*. I really needed to ask, "Who do I need to BECOME?" At that moment, I made a major transition in my life.

I decided that I was going to do whatever it took to become a man who was unshakably confident. Rather than trying to figure out a formula for achieving success and satisfaction, I vowed to find out what I was made of – to test my limits, challenge preconceived notions, and set a new standard for what I no longer accepted from myself. I made up my mind that life would have no choice but to yield to what I wanted if I became someone powerful enough to demand it. So I began my search for something to lean on that could withstand tremendous pressure and the inevitable challenges I would face during my journey.

I realized that in order to completely rebuild myself, I would have to set aside time to take a good hard look at myself. I needed to figure out what truly mattered to me instead of what society was asking of me. I needed to find out what I wanted to make my main purpose in life, and what I was willing to do to make it happen. I had to ultimately rewrite the script I had created for myself and replace it with something more substantial.

I spent years transforming my inner blueprint and beliefs, eventually flipping hundreds of switches of limiting self-beliefs and fears. Ironically, the steps I took often led me to failure and embarrassment, but failing over and over again allowed me to learn from my mistakes and grow stronger. Throughout this process, I documented every new discovery I made in a journal and applied what I was learning as often as I could.

However, I wasn't able to really take my life to the next level until I started studying and coaching with men who were extremely charismatic and confident. I modeled world-class public speakers and distilled their wisdom into powerful communication techniques. I duplicated the body language and vocal tonalities of dynamic media personalities. I emulated a warrior mindset of integrity and determination from a Zen master and lucrative entrepreneur. I received weekly coaching from a kung fu expert and multimillionaire. My personality rapidly shifted from spending days, weeks, and months with these champions, and I witnessed my self-concept evolve far beyond what I could have ever imagined.

With this knowledge in mind, I felt a burning desire to share as much as I could with the world and help men who were struggling with what I had been through. I begin sharing this expertise on self-confidence as a certified life coach, working one on one with my clients to help them achieve their goals and dreams. To this day, I have found my greatest gifts in empowering others to access a stronger vision for who they are by teaching what I know about social influence, creating attraction, and discovering greater happiness in life.

My mission is to not only share the concepts that will increase your self-esteem, but to also show you a process for living a much richer life. I don't intend for you to have a little more swagger, project a little more confidence, and then leave you to fill in the blanks. My mission is to help you develop the courage to go after every endeavor you choose with tenacity and expectations of success and fulfillment.

Because I've been there, I've felt your frustration, and I know there is more to this journey than settling for anything less than you're capable of achieving.

A Common Struggle

I don't know exactly where you're coming from - whether you're struggling with relationships, shyness, social anxiety, making friends and meeting people, or if you simply would like to sharpen your personality and become more likeable and magnetic.

But if you've ever spent time thinking about creating lasting change in who you are and what you're getting out of life, we're on the same page. If you've ever been dissatisfied with how you feel about yourself and how others respond to you, this book is exactly what you're looking for. Whether you have spent nights alone and miserable or even just a few moments frustrated and yearning for more, you're going to move forward with powerful solutions.

There's something I've discovered while spending time on this planet:

Everybody dies. This is a natural fact we can't avoid. **But not everyone lives**. Most people fail to fulfill their expectations and allow their ideal selves to remain a distant dream.

You need to realize that you are important and life is far too short to spend it frustrated with your stake in the world. You need to fight for what's valuable to you and honor your highest potential. Anything short of that means you're not making the most of your time on Earth.

It Starts With You

So what's YOUR story? What are you struggling with right now? How do you see yourself on a daily basis?

As you read Unshakable Swagger, you're going to come across a lot of suggestions for altering a mindset or implementing a new habit. You may face resistance, telling yourself, "I'm too _____ for that." This is your STORY. You might have a few that rattle around in your mind while reading the book. They sound like:

6

"I'm just a _____ - there's no way I can do that."

"I don't have enough _____ to pull off something like that."

"That's for other people, not for someone like me."

"I'm not cool/good/smart/young/old enough to do that."

If your weight, height, intelligence, age, physical looks, experience, or social status are part of the rationale behind why you're not confident, understand something big:

You're not giving yourself permission to get what you want. Your story is keeping you CONSISTENT with the IDENTITY you have created for yourself. It keeps you from growing, stretching your possibilities, and transforming your personality. This is the very thing that keeps you stuck.

The time has come for you look at the excuses you've been making and face them with courage. If you know what your story is, I suggest you write it down right now. Putting pen to paper makes it tangible and allows you to disassociate yourself from it.

My story (or biggest excuse for not getting what I want in life) is:

_____

_____

_____

If you're not quite sure what's holding you back, pay attention to any resistance you feel to trying new things - especially what you're terrified of. Ask yourself, "Why don't I see myself doing that?" Acknowledge these limitations; don't ignore them and continue reading. Face the excuses you're making and then challenge them. There is absolutely nothing and no one holding you back from transformation...except you.

I want to share a simple idea with you that if taken to heart, can revolutionize your life:

It is possible to cultivate an unflappable level of confidence that transcends any fears, doubts, and anxieties you may have about yourself. You can feel completely at ease, become the party everywhere you go, and demand respect in every room you walk into from this moment forward. You can in fact just be a "regular guy" with no special talents, connections, or wealth and have all of the fun and adventure you want in your life. You only need to simply accept this and wipe out any disempowering beliefs that state otherwise.

You're about to find out how to create a much larger blueprint for what's possible in your life. We're not just going to cover the outer skills and strategies for building social influence. We're going to dive in deep to discover who you really are and how to access a hidden power that has been buried inside you. This book is about becoming a bigger man, expanding how you think about yourself and your relationship with the world. The good news is that no matter how shy, introverted, quiet, awkward, or weak you feel you are right now, your current self pales in comparison to who you have the potential of evolving into by applying the concepts from what you're about to read.

Let's kick this thing off by shattering some misconceptions and discover what Unshakable Swagger *is NOT made of.*

 Common Misconceptions

I like to call these the "social shortcuts" for obtaining confidence. A person can indeed feel better about himself for having or expressing these things, but they are all temporary solutions that often dissolve quickly.

Unshakable Swagger is Not Something You Can Buy

True confidence does not come from having the nice clothes, the expensive car, the glorious bachelor pad, or the extravagant toys. While they certainly make nice additions to a man's lifestyle, they do not define his value. What you have the ability to purchase ultimately says little to nothing about your character.

Now I'm not advocating that the ownership of trendy clothes, sexy cars, or expensive gadgets is a *bad* thing. I'm saying that hanging one's self-confidence on them is a fallacy and not a substitute for healthy self-esteem. Unshakable Swagger does not come from exchanging dollars for status; you can't buy your way to confidence.

You cannot be a powerful, collected individual who believes the key to your happiness and respect lies in showing off what you own. When you attach your identity to these things, your entire self-concept crumbles as soon as their novelty fades. When what you own isn't cool anymore or, God forbid, you can't afford it any longer, you're left chasing after a new security blanket to cling to. This is like building a house on top of a mountain of sand - the more superficial your foundation is, the more likely you'll fall apart as times change.

Seek wealth not from a place of showing off to the world or trying to prove how valuable you are, but rather as a gift from hard work and authentic passion.

Unshakable Swagger is Not Being Better Than Others

Unshakable Swagger is not boasting about how powerful you are to others and it's *definitely* not cutting the people around you down to make you feel better about yourself.

Unfortunately, this misconception probably ranks the highest. If you look up the dictionary definition of swagger, here's what you get:

"an ostentatious display of arrogance and conceit."

Now I'm not one to dispute the freakin' dictionary but I have to whole-heartedly disagree about this. Being arrogant and conceited means a person is operating under the assumption that they are *better* than someone else.

Here are the facts:

No one is better than you and you are no better than anyone else. We're all EQUAL.

No matter how loudly you may proclaim your brilliance, display your conquering of opponents, or demand attention for your accomplishments, every single person on this planet is worth exactly as much as you are.

In fact, it's a mark of enormous insecurity to feel the need to behave this way. What you're really doing is broadcasting the message that you're not confident enough in your own value for others to naturally observe it. And in demolishing someone else's confidence, you fool yourself into appearing to be stronger. Sadly, many people think the fastest way to feel powerful in a given situation is to chop others down.

Arrogant people make the critical mistake in assuming they receive more respect and admiration for this behavior. In reality, they tend to be alienated quickly for their selfish attention and incessant need to draw a reaction from others.

On the flip side, being overly modest is not the solution either. You must stand firm in your power and not back down when challenged. You'll learn several examples of how to do this throughout the book. For now, it's sufficient to know that it's important to find the proper balance between hitting everyone over the head with how great you are and shying away from the spotlight to hide and play small.

Unshakable Swagger is Not Confined to What You Look Like

We live in a world that grossly operates under the notion of "I'll believe it when I see it." We assume that the reality around us dictates our beliefs (and not the other way around).

Here's what I mean: when we think of someone who seems cool and has his stuff together, we think, "Hey this guy looks cool – he must be confident." What doesn't cross our minds is, "Hey this guy's confident – that's *why* he looks cool." What we SEE on the outside seems to dictate our beliefs.

In actuality, it is our beliefs that determine the reality we see around us. Instead of worrying about solely focusing on what you look like and what others see when they're around you, I suggest you shift internally and start focusing on your own thoughts, emotions, and beliefs regarding you and the world. Looking sharp and crisp is only the tip of the iceberg, and with fashion trends in constant flux, you're better off improving what you're going to take around with you your entire life: your mindset.

I'll discuss clothing and style and how they play a role later on in the book. To be certain, what you wear has an effect on how you feel. But the key takeaway is to realize that it barely affects your confidence if you're built from the inside-out. You can even be described as "ugly" or "goofy" or "average in every way" and take over a party, make tons of friends, and have the time of your life with anyone you desire.

The key lies in building your blueprint up to the point where you feel completely comfortable in any given situation and believe that no matter what someone says or does to you, how you think about yourself never changes.

Keep this in mind: seeing is not believing. BELIEVING is SEEING.

Unshakable Swagger is Not About Your Social Connections

Raise your hand if you went to college with someone who wouldn't let more than five minutes of conversation go by without referencing the fact that his family was part of the university's legacy. Bonus round: raise both hands if you knew someone who seemed to be the life of the party with his fraternity brothers but acted strangely quiet and unsure on his own.

There are many people in groups or clubs who so strongly associate with their membership that if they were to be stripped of their status, they wouldn't know how to identify themselves anymore. Or worse, if their club were to be criticized or attacked, they would react emotionally, as if the critique was directed at them specifically.

Think of how passionate our country is about sports. When a person identifies strongly with a sports team, he refers to the team as "we." "WE played well last week." "WE suck." As if this person has any impact whatsoever on the team's performance. What's funny to me is how this intense passion can quickly turn to anger when fans of opposing team begin arguing with one another. There's such a deep-rooted attachment to sports organizations that if you're attacking a man's team, you might as well be attacking him and his family. This is known as GROUPTHINK.

I spent some time living in Los Angeles and it was quite an experience. The Hollywood culture is highly obsessed with image. Out there, it's not just how you look that seems to matter, but who you are "seen with." Hollywood has a habit of what they call "name dropping." It loves mentioning celebrities or famous persons in an effort to prove popularity and being "in the know" to others. The popular mindset there seems to be: "Hey – you must think I'm pretty awesome to be hanging out with X Celebrity, don't you?"

Once again, this is another example of trying to leverage social status for confidence. Instead of feeling naturally great about himself, your typical guy will try to prove his greatness by pointing out whom he knows. As long as his membership in the group is active and others know of his status, he believes he has the right to feel good about himself. But what happens when the group falls apart or he loses access?

It's not pretty.

Unshakable Swagger is Not About Your Sexual Exploits

Right off the bat, let me address what you may be thinking: "Are you suggesting we don't go out and get laid?"

The answer is no. DUH.

What I'm saying is to not be so obsessed with sex that it completely dictates how you think about yourself.

Men have a natural desire to attach sexual conquest with identity. If other guys find out that we're not going out and having sex, we're immediately harassed and belittled. The day after our first date with a woman, our friends probably only want to know one thing. Hint: it's not what restaurant you took her to. More often than not, this is just how we operate. Believe me, I get it.

But we've placed such a high importance on the act of having sex and letting others know about it that we're objectifying our relationships with women and letting them dictate our self-esteem and happiness.

Here's the problem: if you attach any feelings of self-confidence towards your sexual behavior, you're essentially placing all of your power into the approval of women. You'll see the process of dating play out as an attempt for you to "sell" yourself in order to win her over. This shows up whenever you try to overtly impress her by showing off the cool/expensive stuff you own, the amount of money in your bank account, the exclusive club you're apart of, or the special people you know.

Any of that sound familiar?

When you occur to yourself as a naturally attractive guy who offers just as much value to a woman as you receive from her, you won't feel the need to consider members of the opposite sex as "conquests." You won't be attaching your ego to the activity of having sex and, once again, you'll prove to have a ton more going for you than just this one area of your life.

Women know every time if you are pursuing them in order to feel better about yourself. It's one of the fastest ways to discredit yourself and for her to lose all respect for you. Conversely, if you approach a girl with the mindset of "I'm an incredible guy with a lot to share," you will have an infinitely easier time dating and handling relationships.

My Definition

OK...so you have a pretty solid handle on what it isn't...so what *is* Unshakable Swagger?

Here's how I see it:

Unshakable Swagger is an internal feeling you exude that naturally attracts and pulls people into your reality. It's a way of living, breathing, and moving that works from the inside-out. It is BELIEVING you are valuable, worthy of success, and capable of handling adversity that results in others SEEING you as popular, confident, and charismatic.

It means giving yourself the permission to aggressively pursue anything you desire in life. It is being your own best friend and biggest source of inspiration, courage, and determination. It is a lifestyle you create and continuously expand to operate at the highest standard you can possibly set.

At the end of the day, it's looking at yourself in the mirror without hiding or making excuses for the man you are. It is about taking complete responsibility for your beliefs, actions, and behaviors – owning the choices you make throughout life to shape who you become.

Unshakable Swagger is about speaking your mind freely and with authenticity even when your truth might clash with what others are thinking. This means approving of yourself and what you really believe in comes as a far higher priority than seeking acceptance from others. It's an unconditional, rock-solid confidence that transcends any situation you may encounter.

When you possess Unshakable Swagger, there is literally nothing that can damage your self-esteem. You are free to move through life without the fear of making mistakes or being humiliated. In this sense, you're completely at ease with your relationship to the world. Your identity is never under threat or at risk for embarrassment – no matter where you are or what you're doing, you own the belief that you're just fine.

You can still have everything we discussed that doesn't define swagger; in fact, it's easier to attract more money, the perfect woman for you, and a significant social circle if you think of these things as the EFFECTS of who you are (and not the required possessions you need to feel good about yourself).

Why Unshakable Swagger is Important

You should have realized by now that I'm not just going to give you a few quick tips here or there on acting cool. By the time you're done reading this, you're going to know more than most people ever will about creating an unwavering sense of trust in yourself and who you are.

You may be thinking, "Yeah...so why is any of this stuff important?" Why not just hand out a few quick tips on charisma and social skills and send you on your way? Why not just get you a few more dates, make a few more friends, be a little more popular, and just be done with it?

Well, because this isn't just a luxury or something nice to have. Unshakable Swagger is becoming increasingly necessary as we have to rely more on our own judgment and trust in ourselves to lead our own lives. With an ever-expanding list of choices and options available to us, we are now living in what author and psychologist T. George Harris calls "The Era of Conscious Choice."[1] We have to make decisions about tons of things in today's world that previous generations either didn't have to make or already had laid out for them.

We're free to decide who we want to marry or even *if* we want to marry. How many kids we'd like to have or *if* we even want kids. Where we want to live – in the city, suburbs, tucked away from society...overseas, in America, Europe, or elsewhere. We can choose a religion we'd like to study or if we'd like to have any religion at all. We can decide to earn a living – working a job for someone else or starting off on our own as entrepreneurs.

And of course, we have millions upon millions of options regarding how we want to spend our free time, our money, and our energy. A hoard of products competes for our attention, a never-ending ocean of resources exists for our entertainment, and all of this information creates thousands of tiny decisions we need to make on a daily basis. Never before has any civilization seen so much freedom of choice available.

At the same time, we've got a lot of responsibility on our shoulders. To truly succeed and feel happy with all of these decisions, we must know who we are, what we value, and what matters to us. We need to be able to depend on ourselves to cultivate our own resources and trust others to help when we come up short.

Without having a firm grasp on these things, a man can feel like he's floating through the ocean at high tide. He's more likely to be manipulated, exploited, weakened, embarrassed, and damaged if he's not consciously shaping who he is and what he believes in. Without solid ground to stand on, he'll find it's all too easy to get pushed over or taken advantage of.

Rock-solid confidence is the ROOT of all happiness and success in life. There is nothing more important than possessing complete assurance in your capabilities. If you lack self-reliance on any level, it will always show up and rear its ugly head. Your job interviews will fall flat, your relationships will crumble, your income will suffer, and your overall enjoyment from life will be less than half of what it could be. Choosing to not address any feelings of inferiority is equal to choosing boredom and frustration over fulfillment and excitement.

In life, we don't always get what we WANT. More often that not, we get what we ARE. The world you see around you on a daily basis is a reflection of your deepest beliefs. If these beliefs are weak and limited, your reality will be full of pain, suffering, and a sense of not getting what you want. If, however, your beliefs are empowering and unshakable, your life will be rich with incredible opportunities, people, and happiness. It all comes down to you.

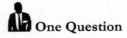 One Question

So here's what all of this boils down to: one question only you can answer.

Are you *committed* to change?

Are you open to growing your mind, body, and spirit in new and uncomfortable ways? Are you truly open to the idea of leaving your old self behind and taking on new behaviors, beliefs, and habits? Are you hungry enough to desire increase in your life or are you totally content with where you are now?

I'm assuming that since you bought this book and invested in your growth, the answer to these questions is yes. But I didn't just ask if you WANT to change. I asked if you're COMMITTED.

There's a world of difference between these ideas. Everyone wants to change but few are truly committed. Having an awareness that you'd like to change is only the first step; the rest is based on consistent ACTION. Remember, you can be as confident and have as much adventure and excitement in your life as you want. However, reading this book by itself won't be enough – you must apply these concepts even when you feel strange, afraid, or not in the mood to try them.

With that being said, you might come across a few ideas or concepts you already know when you read the following pages. But I'm not concerned with how much you already know; I only care about what you LIVE. Rather than skimming ahead to a later section, allow everything you read that you already know to be seen as a reminder to live a more involved life. When you discover a brand new idea, test it in reality as soon as you have the chance to do so. Make a promise to infuse the following information into as many opportunities you find as possible. By doing this, you lock the material deep into your subconscious mind.

If you're committed to grabbing these lessons by the horns and never letting go, you will have lasting confidence – in fact, as much as you want in spades. If you hold onto this belief and stop at nothing to consistently develop and push yourself, there is no limit I or anyone else can ever place on you. You will realize there are no longer any rules or regulations blocking you from what you want. The world has always been yours to claim.

The choice is yours: you can take action on what you learn or you can file this book away with the other "good reading material."

Choose wisely.

2

CDC: CENTER FOR DAMAGED CONFIDENCE

"If I have lost confidence in myself, I have the universe against me." – Emerson

This is what I call the "Healing Chapter." They say all healing must start with awareness – so I thought it would be fitting to walk you through a brief but comprehensive guide to why you're probably not as confident as you want to be.

In order to give you some leverage and a higher consciousness about what has previously determined how confident (or unconfident) you are, we're going to discuss the most powerful factors that have influenced the way you think about yourself.

Welcome to the Center for Damaged Confidence. The doctor will be right with you.

In this chapter, you'll learn:

- How society has conditioned you to live in fear and place limits on what you are capable of achieving

- How your mind works to sabotage you from getting what you want

- Exactly where you might have holes in your self-esteem and how to begin filling them

 ## Social Conditioning

You were born for the most part as a totally clean slate; you came into the world with only a few instincts guiding your decisions. As you grew into your childhood, teenage years, and then adult life, you began taking on beliefs, ideas, and truisms taught to you by society. This process, known as social conditioning, educated you so that you didn't have to learn everything for yourself firsthand.

This is usually extremely helpful; being taught that certain activities have dangerous and life-threatening consequences saves us from risking death to find out. We know to not touch hot surfaces because our parents taught us that doing so would result in immense pain. We've learned much of our values from social conditioning as well – what society passes down to us often guides our lives. Good habits such as saving your money, being good to others, and working hard have beneficial effects.

However, there are many beliefs and values you were taught that do not serve to empower you. They were often delivered with good intentions but many resulted in you growing up to behave with far less strength and self-assurance than you could have. At its best, social conditioning simplifies life's most important lessons for our benefit. However at its worst, it creates a reliance on what others think and a hesitance to act in accordance with one's own intuition.

Here are the four biggest ways a person receives this conditioning throughout life:

By Your Parents

Ah, yes, the classic choice. "It's all my parents' fault. Let's just blame them for everything!" Book complete...my work here is done!

Not so fast. Before we get into this section, let's preface the obvious: your parents did the best job they could in raising you. They took all of the information they were given and gave it their best shot to the greatest of their abilities. So unless you come from a *really* damaged family, your parents' intentions were to help you become an independent, healthy adult. Unfortunately, there are several concepts they trained and drilled into your head repeatedly that did far more harm than good.

Have you ever heard a mother yelling at her child, saying things like:

"NO!"

"BE CAREFUL!"

"DON'T!"

"STOP!"

Of course you have. A mother focuses incessantly on ensuring a child's safety; obviously it is one of her highest priorities. The polar opposite of this type of behavior would be someone like Casey Anthony, a mother who at the very least neglected her own daughter's safety and at the very worst was responsible for her death. No mother in her right mind would ever want to be viewed as lackadaisical about her offspring's health but what results is often a borderline obsession with safety.

This "safety obsession" is often overbearing and entirely too strict. It restricts the kid from taking chances and learning about the impact of cause and effect. If a child is not allowed to play on his own, make mistakes, and get banged up from time to time, he won't learn about taking risks. If he's too sheltered and protected from taking these risks, how is he expected to develop assertiveness? And even more importantly, how is he supposed to

21

be able to challenge himself and feel what's it like to conquer adversity?

An example of this is when a kid walks along the edge of a brick wall for fun. Let's say his mother sees this and quickly tells him to get down because he'll fall and break his neck (as opposed to simply monitoring him). So the child reluctantly slows down, gets scooped up by his mom, and returns safely to lower heights. If this kind of behavior plays out in a similar fashion over and over again, the less space he will be given to challenge his courage and approach danger. Naturally, he'll become conditioned to playing it safe because he is rewarded for doing so and punished for disobeying. Over time, the fear of heights will slowly but surely find its way into his subconscious until one day he wakes up scared of falling from tall places.

I have a six-year-old nephew who thinks it would be a great idea to leap off the balcony of his father's fifth story condo into a community swimming pool below. The kid is absolutely fearless when it comes to heights (just not always the most rational decision maker I know). My point isn't to say that children should be left to wander the planet and fend for themselves or to say that parents should allow a kid to risk serious injury. I'm saying there is a balance between keeping the little dude protected and letting him get his wings.

Here's the key point:

When the balance leans too heavily toward safety and comfort, it teaches him that: 1) taking action and stepping out of his comfort zone is WRONG because 2) the very act of doing it will result in FAILURE or PAIN. As Nathaniel Branden observes in his book *The Six Pillars of Self-Esteem*: "If a child is chastised for making a mistake, or ridiculed, humiliated, or punished – or if the parent steps in impatiently and says, 'Here, let me do it!' - he or she cannot feel free to struggle and learn. A natural process of growth is sabotaged. To avoid mistakes becomes a higher priority than to master new challenges."[2]

Read that back to yourself a second time and think about the consequences this behavior may have had on your life. Was there a specific time when you wanted to step out of your comfort zone and try new things but you were absolutely convinced you would fail or humiliate yourself if you tried? Was there a beautiful girl you desperately wanted to talk to in order to ask out on a date but felt like doing so would be a waste of time because you were positive she'd reject you? You can probably come up with hundreds of examples. Thinking back, there have been literally thousands of moments like these strewn across my life.

There are moments in life so critical to our self-esteem and identity that shying away from them stunts our personal growth dramatically. These moments ALWAYS contain risk, danger, and the threat of embarrassment or physical pain on some level. Backing down from these opportunities kills off the potential for independence and instead breeds a higher degree of dependence on those we know we're safe with.

The older you get, the more debilitating this gets; becoming a MAN is IMPOSSIBLE if you are terrified of facing the unknown and handling adversity.

This might just be the biggest reason why you're not as confident as you'd like to be.

By the Media

Society has placed and continues to place a high value on conspicuous consumption – that what we buy greatly determines our self-worth. You've actually been conditioned throughout your entire life to believe that these things will lead to making you feel better about who you are.

How do I know this? Think about how many advertisements you see in a given day. Even if you do your best to avoid watching television, stay away from Youtube, and "unplug" from the digital world entirely, you're being constantly targeted for endless marketing. In many restaurants, it's impossible to even use the restroom without seeing something vying for your attention. In fact, the average person may receive over 5000 advertisements a day in some form or another.

Yes, five <u>thousand</u>.

Now, I'm no psychologist, but I can take a stab at what the aim and purpose of a typical commercial is (and I think you'll agree with me): to motivate you to buy a product. To achieve this, the agency or persons responsible for crafting the campaign must possess some knowledge of psychology and influence. If their message does not motivate enough people to purchase the product or at least become aware of it, the campaign fails.

Back when the media first began running television commercials in the early 1940's, the strategy utilized was pretty straightforward. You can imagine a small board room meeting with men in grey suits getting together and crafting a twenty to thirty second spot that simply let the viewer know about the product and a few key reasons to buy it.

As the next few decades progressed, our media began getting more and more sophisticated. With viewers becoming jaded with old methods and strategies, an increased efficiency in impacting the audience was necessary. Psychology began playing a bigger and bigger role; now it wasn't just about telling someone to buy the product. It was about hitting his "hot buttons" - sex, power, death, fame, and status to shock his subconscious into taking action.

The underlying message in most of this information is a simple one that we're mostly not conscious of: without X product in your life, you will suffer and with X product in your life, you will be happy. We've become so jaded to ad campaigns that when reading what I just wrote, you probably said, "duh." Consciously, most people know the purpose and impact of commercials, but subconsciously they aren't aware of how much it is programming their beliefs. They assume that being exposed to all of this has no effect on their belief system, blissfully unaware that the conclusions they may be drawing from life are in fact illusions. You know, it's called TV *programming* for a reason.

Have you ever thought about why you purchase a certain car over others? Is it really because you logically chose the *best* vehicle or because you associate having a higher status, more sex appeal, and being generally liked by others more because of it? Even if you haven't had the luxury of buying a car that fits your criteria, think about your dream car. Is it your ideal car because it excels in performing its primary function or because it enhances your self-concept?

I understand that people buy things for different reasons. You may be the type of person who rarely (if ever) purchase new products based on these parameters. I realize that people don't buy dish soap in order to feel better about themselves. But in some way or another, you've been strongly motivated to base most of your purchasing habits on this idea. You have been conditioned, whether you like it or not, to believe your happiness and self-concept can be greatly affected by what you buy.

Think about how powerful it is to see a celebrity endorsing a particular product. Do you believe that people are choosing to spend money on what he or she is promoting because it is the best product available in the market or because they resonate with the celebrity's fame, power, and sex appeal? One single person with high status can start entire consumption movements. They can largely and quickly influence what members of the general public consider "cool" and "hip" and feel they must buy to stay current.

There are countless more ways that the media programs your thoughts and beliefs, but this isn't a psychology textbook. The main point to take home here is that *the media motivates you to seek self-confidence and happiness from a source outside of yourself.*

By School

Here's a familiar mantra:

Get good grades...so you can get into a good college...so you can get good grades... so you can get into a good graduate program...so you can get good grades...so you can get a good job.

Heard that one before?

As a kid, it seemed like EVERYONE was obsessed with grades. Supposedly, they were the golden key to unlocking the combination to a happy life. If you received bad grades in school, you must have been a stupid, lazy, or uncommitted student – which would mean you wouldn't get into a good college – which would mean you wouldn't get a good job – which would mean you would end up an unhappy loser.

Just think about how much pressure you were under (or may still be under) to get good marks. In our culture, slipping on an assignment or test doesn't just mean you made a few mistakes. It means FAILURE. You might as well have the Scarlet Letter tattooed to your chest if you bring home an 'F' to your parents. If your family was invested in your success at school, there were extremely harsh consequences to poor grades.

Let's take a look at the damage this can do to your subconscious mind. Getting anything less than an 'A' means you're WRONG on some level. There really is no gray area here; you're either correct or incorrect. What do you think this does to your desire to take chances and risks? Do you really want to go out on a limb with this much on the line? The formula we had drilled into our heads over and over again was:

Making MISTAKES = BAD and leads to PAIN.

The implications of the grading system suggest that there is no room for trial and error. You either get the questions right the first time or face severe consequences. There is no chance to experiment with different solutions and learn from our own mistakes. This translates into post-graduate life in several ways: we're far less likely to stray from doing what we're good at, we stick to our comfort zone so that we don't have to endure the damning sense of failure, and we quit pursuits at the first sign of difficulty because making mistakes is too painful.

With the stakes always being high, going to school motivated us to become outcome-oriented and not process-oriented. We were rewarded all the same no matter how much studying or work was done to get the 'A.' A more gifted student could spend five minutes studying for a test while another five hours and there was absolutely no discrepancy in the value of the final grade. Whether or not the kid worked his tail off throughout school or not, at the end of the day, his final scorecard was all that mattered.

Ask yourself, were you truly interested in learning as much as you could about the Pythagorean Theorem or whether or not you could

26

just put down the correct answers on paper and move on? I'll admit that I cheated on large homework assignments a few times in high school because I simply had no desire to take the time required to produce the correct answers. I saw absolutely no motivation to actually master the concepts being taught. If the grade was all that mattered, why should I care about the process of learning?

The problem with this way of thinking is that it is entirely counter-intuitive to self-growth. If I am tackling a new project or learning a new hobby and am obsessed with my results, something very frustrating begins to happen when I'm not getting the outcomes I'm looking for. Practicing and trying again just leads to more pain and failure as mistakes are made repeatedly. I'm motivated to want to just throw the whole thing out the window and quit.

But if I'm not attached to my temporary results – if I'm more concerned with the process as a whole, I can concentrate on making small adjustments and will naturally move closer to mastery. The "failures" I encounter no longer equate to pain; instead, they are the necessary feedback I need to improve. Over time, the thousands of hours of practice I put in will add up to the results I was looking for all along.

If you are afraid of failure and have trouble tolerating mistakes from yourself, consider that anything you desire worthy of your time will always include both. In fact, if you are not failing every now and then, it's a strong sign you're not truly serious about what you're pursuing. Instead of striving to be a perfectionist who tiptoes around potential failure, embrace your errors; they are designed to help you master what you're learning.

Everything Else

Of course there are many more ways we are socially conditioned. Political affiliations, strict religious doctrines, peer pressure, and government legislation may all have an effect on how we perceive the world. It would be impossible for me to fully cover this topic without extending the book to 400+ pages. I think you get the point.

Here's something really important to consider: were you ever taught, at any point in your life, how to:

- Find love and create lasting relationships

- Become happy

- Love who you are

- Conquer your fears

- Live a balanced and successful life

No? You mean your parents didn't hand down these crucial ideas to you? You didn't take a class in Personal Happiness 101? But you learned all about the War of 1812 – didn't *that* shape your values and principles?

Most people have an extremely shallow idea of who they are, what they truly want, and what actually motivates them to do go after it. The sad thing is these very people refuse to question the confidence-shattering conditioning fed to them by society throughout their lives, such as:

"Be realistic – you're not going to get all that you want."

"You need to lower your expectations – life doesn't work like that."

"You can't do that. It's impossible."

"If you don't do what we tell you, you're making a huge mistake."

We obviously need our parents to help shape our values and keep us protected from danger. We need school to educate us so that we might understand how the world works and without the media or advertising, our economy would surely collapse. However, we have to wake up to the debilitating beliefs we're downloading into our brains and begin defining what truth is to each of us *individually*. It's time to wipe the dirt and debris off the windshield so we can discern the best road we wish to take.

 **The Conditioned Mind**

So based on what we just covered, you could just blame society for all of your shortcomings and frustrations and build a massive case for lashing out against anyone or anything that has contributed to your suffering. But let's not start blaming others for the way things are. Let's take a deeper look inside the way your brain operates so we understand how it also may have created some thoughts of inferiority.

For a belief to be communicated, it must first be accepted or agreed on at some level. Consciously or unconsciously, you accepted the beliefs that were shared with you from society. These thoughts are almost always accepted at a young age, especially when these three factors fall into place:

1. Repetition – Hearing the same information over and over again

2. Intensity – The more the information has an emotional impact on you, the deeper it is imprinted

3. Authority – We almost always accept information from authority figures we trust

You can see why you accepted so much of what you were taught as a child without question – you heard the same lessons several times, there were immense consequences for betraying what you were taught, and you looked up to your parents and teachers for guidance. Your mind soaked up almost everything it was taught without the capability to discriminate what was false or disempowering.

While the vast majority of your strongest beliefs were shaped during this time, you also carry around a lot of limiting beliefs about yourself based on past experience. You've undoubtedly cultivated a long list of habits, convictions, and preferences that affect the daily choices you make. Over time, your mind created a specific blueprint for your unique status quo – the way things are and the way things "should be" - even if the blueprint limits you.

So what happens when you become aware of these limitations and try to change them? Resistance sets in. Your mind has become CONDITIONED to maintain the status quo of your beliefs so your self-concept is never questioned. When you attempt to take on new habits or beliefs, your brain literally sabotages these efforts because they don't show up anywhere in your mental blueprint.

This is where your STORY shows up as you find yourself saying things like, "That's not me" or "I'm not good enough to do this." The conditioned mind hardens you from self-examination, and blocks you from believing you can change and expand your blueprint. It knows exactly what thoughts to feed you to keep you comfortable right where you are. Change or growth on any level is the conditioned mind's enemy; unknown territory contains new experiences it's not accustomed to.

Without having both the awareness and the desire to move past old conditioning, you are doomed to repeat the same cycle on endless repeat. Your story will always stop you from going after your goals and trying new things. For most people, their lives are permanently wrapped up in the same limiting beliefs they refuse to let go.

How can you tell when you're allowing your conditioned mind to call the shots? Simple – any time you don't show up with what you said you would do – especially when you make excuses for not following through on actions that would bring you more happiness. Here's a profound choice you're going to have to make: you can either have successes or you can have rationalizations. You can't have both; you either justify why you're unable to achieve something or you simply go do it.

Fortunately, every time you take action in spite of your excuses, your conditioned mind's influence weakens. You advance beyond the disempowering story you believe that shackles you to your comfort zone. Each time you venture into uncharted territory and successfully achieve something new, you trust in a higher sense of guidance. I'll be exploring this with more detail in the next chapter.

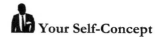 **Your Self-Concept**

Your self-concept is the map of how you see yourself and your relation to the world – your sense of value, worth, sex appeal, intelligence, work ethic, and so on. Whether or not you feel confident in a given set of circumstances depends squarely on your self-concept. You won't boldly move forward with something if your self-concept doesn't match up with it.

In fact, you will always behave like the person you perceive yourself to be. You cannot achieve lasting success in anything without first believing you are a person who is capable of doing it.

This is why it's very difficult to just suddenly "act confident" in a situation in which you bring an unconfident identity to the table. Any feel-good book that tells you to "fake it 'til you make it" misses the point; you can fake it all you want to, but deep down, if your identity is not rooted in beliefs about yourself that reflect positive expectation and strength, your confidence fades almost immediately.

Everything you are "good" at doing come from a positive self-concept. Conversely, everything you are "bad" at doing come from a negative self-concept. You can look at any area of your life and check out the results you're getting and trace it back to an aspect of your sense of self. If a possible result matches up with what you suspect to be true about yourself, you will accept it without question. Likewise, if a potential result does NOT match up with what you suspect to be true, you will reject it (for better or worse).

This is why the majority of people that win the lottery end up losing all of the money. The outer result (money) doesn't match up with the inner mindset (self-concept). The mind then self-sabotages relentlessly until they are back to square one.

If you are dating a woman you believe to be "out of your league," you might subconsciously find ways to sabotage the relationship. You'll believe you don't deserve her, so you will question the validity of you two being together. You'll worry about her cheating, think something in her is flawed because she's with you, and chase

31

her away to stay consistent with your beliefs about yourself. While on the surface this may sound ridiculous, it's one of the most prominent examples of how a weak self-concept can destroy anything good in your life.

Understanding the direct relationship between your self-concept and the world around you is a critical component of Unshakable Swagger. The more clear you are about the negative and damaging beliefs you have about WHO you ARE, the more efficiently you're able to wipe them out and get what you WANT. Remember, we don't get what we want in life - we get what we are.

Self-Esteem

Self-esteem, or the amount of love and respect you have for yourself, can be described in a multitude of ways. Any belief you have about yourself stems from your self-esteem. However, there are four main aspects that directly affect your overall sense of happiness and success in life. Thomas Howell, author of *You Are the Creator of Your Life*, describes them as:

- Wisdom – how smart, creative, logical, wise, and intuitive you think you are

- Power – how capable, strong, responsible, and powerful you think you are

- Value – how good, valuable, worthy, important, and deserving you think you are

- Love – how respected, appreciated, loved, and admired you think you are (and especially how much you love yourself)[3]

Some of the most painful moments in your life more than likely concerned you feeling particularly weak about one (or several) of these identities. For example, going through an unexpected breakup is extraordinarily painful because all four areas are affected; your wisdom takes a hit because you didn't see it coming; your power weakens because the decision was made without your consent; your value plunges because she doesn't wish to invest more of her time with you; and your love dwindles because you're clearly not as loved or admired as you once thought you were.

Conversely, your happiest moments in life occur when you feel these identities strengthen. When you receive promotions at work, hear a girl accept your offer for a date, win a close competition, or even predict the final score of a sports game, your sense of self rises. The more actions you take that increase how you think of yourself in regards to these identities, the more your confidence will grow.

With this in mind, you must be aware of any beliefs of unworthiness you have regarding success or happiness. Take a few minutes right now and consider how confident you feel in regards to your wisdom, power, value, and love. Rate yourself 1-10 in each area:

- Wisdom _____/10

- Power _____/10

- Value_____/10

- Love_____/10

You can't display unflinching swagger if you still harbor deeply rooted feelings of inferiority in regards to any of these concepts. Ask yourself this: what ONE belief do I have about myself that stops me from believing I'm a 10 out of 10?

Damaged Self-Esteem

Many people grow into adulthood with a damaged or "missing" sense of wisdom, power, value, or love. To compensate for this, they chase after fulfillment in external things to feel better. For example, if you grew up with difficult parents who never seemed satisfied with your results, you harnessed a strong sense of "not being enough." To compensate for this lack of value, you probably worked relentlessly to get good grades and to find a well-paying job. The less satisfaction your parents gave you, the more you felt like you had to do to PROVE your sense of value. Unfortunately,

33

no matter how much you seemed to achieve, it probably never really filled this void inside of you.

This is why people cut others down (to regain a sense of power), boast about what they know (to regain a sense of wisdom), and chase after shallow relationships (to regain a sense of love). Almost all of the negative actions people commit to one another are simply responses to feelings of lack and inferiority.

If you truly consider yourself wise, powerful, valuable, and loved, you will never feel a lack of confidence in any situation you wind up in. You won't feel like you have anything to prove. You won't chase after people and things to boost up your self-esteem if you're grounded in total self-acceptance. By really examining these four identities, you can learn a lot about yourself and why you behave the way you do.

Throughout the book, you will see opportunities to enhance your sense of love, power, value, and wisdom. They may come in the form of activities you'll physically do, habits you'll take on, new beliefs you will incorporate, and new ways of interacting with others. The more you read the book and add these suggestions to your life, the more confident you will feel. You're going to be essentially rewiring your beliefs and erasing the stumbling blocks you've placed in your own way.

In order to completely overhaul your self-concept, we need to first lay a new foundation in place that will act as a platform we can build on. The next chapter does just that.

3

BECOME THE WANTED MAN

"There are two questions a man must ask himself. The first is 'Where am I going?' and the second is 'Who will go with me?' If you ever get these questions in the wrong order, you are in trouble."
– Sam Keen

Take your pick of modern comedies – Family Guy, The Simpsons, Two and a Half Men, or any Will Ferrell movie. All of them feature one thing in common: an idiot husband or bachelor with absolutely no idea how to manage his life. We all laugh at these characters' inabilities to balance their work and personal lives because the material rings true.

The men in these shows reflect how stunted many guys are emotionally, mentally, and spiritually. They represent a large chunk of our population who are essentially grown up boys – emotionally immature, still dependent upon the approval of women, and often completely unable to make decisions on their own with assurance.

As a result, they subordinate to their wives, their bosses, and even their parents in order to be accepted.

The problem with living like this is because of how damaging it is to a man's self-reliance. You can't be confident if your wife or girlfriend is wearing the pants in the relationship, calling the shots, and running your life. You can't demand much respect if you're incapable of making decisions without relying on others. You definitely can't feel good about who you are as a man if you're sloppy with your emotions under pressure.

For the most part, this chapter revolves around your confidence with members of the opposite sex, and how being a man is the number one most critical component of healthy relationships. But realize this will also apply to every single aspect of your life as well, especially your demeanor and success in business. This entire chapter is a new foundation for fresh techniques and ideas and will be something you can stand on no matter what situation you find yourself in.

Here's what you can take away from this chapter:

- How to become a powerful, well-balanced man

- The most important concept about attracting women

- How to become mentally stronger and more resilient

- How to successfully leave your comfort zone when necessary

- The importance of integrity

 **Own Your Masculinity**

Whether you're straight, gay, bisexual, or any mixture of the above, there are only two roles you can play in a relationship: masculine or feminine. No matter the situation, one person must take on the masculine role while the other must take on the feminine role. A relationship cannot continue if both are playing the same role.

The problem a lot of men have with dating or relationships altogether is that they end up sliding into too much of the feminine role. If you've heard the old cliché "she's wearing the pants in the relationship," you know what I'm talking about. There are far too many men out there who let women completely dominate their lives because they don't have the inner strength or conviction about who they are and what they want. This is a problem when there are two people both playing the feminine role.

Remember back in high school how the girls were always attracted to the jocks? This is primarily because these guys were more in tune with their masculine side. The manlier a guy is, the more women will tend to be attracted to him. From an evolutionary standpoint, the stronger, more athletic, tougher, and resilient a guy is, the more appealing he is in the eyes of a woman. The more feminine, weaker, uncoordinated, and delicate a guy is, the less appealing he is to a woman. Feminine women simply need a masculine presence to balance their energy.

If a relationship wears on with a guy never stepping up to fulfill his role, his partner will always step into the "man's shoes" to fill in what's missing. As a result, she will lose a vast amount of attraction for him and either leave him, cheat on him, or find some other way to fade out of his life. There are many theories as to why the divorce rate is so high in this country, but I think this is probably the number one biggest reason. Men simply aren't acting like men any more; they're acting like boys who never quite learned what it takes to become a man and own their masculinity.

Author David Deida describes the masculinity a woman yearns for in his book *The Way of the Superior Man*: "She cannot move you, because you already are what you are, with or without her. She cannot scare you away, because you already penetrate her in fearless love, pervading her heart and body. She cannot distract you, because your one-pointed commitment to truth will not bend to her wiles. Feeling this hugeness of love and freedom in you, she can trust you, utterly, and surrender her testing in celebration of love."[4]

37

Let's break down the male gender role you need to fully step into and play to the hilt.

Handle Your Emotions

First of all, you absolutely must have a firm grasp on your emotions. This doesn't mean you bottle your emotions up and go through life as a walking volcano. It means you start learning how to release them in appropriate ways. Whenever you explode in anger and fly off the handle, the respect people have for you plummets. If you get upset easily and start reacting in any context, you will consistently make poor decisions and come across like a child.

You need to be cool, calm, and collected throughout as many of your day-to-day conversations as possible. You'll be operating more from a place of power and clarity if your head isn't clouded by toxic emotions. If you are really pissed off about something, take it out privately on a punching bag or a set of dumbbells. Being angry around other people is an invitation for them to quickly loathe your presence.

There is a Buddhist belief that states we can either utilize our emotions to add value to the world or to destroy it. If I become angry about the injustice a select group of people suffers from and start a fundraising campaign to send them aid, I'm using my anger to add value to the world. If, on the other hand, I yell and scream at my wife for not sharing the same rage and belittle her, I'm being destructive. How you choose to express your emotions tells a great deal about who you are as a man.

Back in hunter-gatherer times, women were looking for PHYSICAL SECURITY from their male partners. The biggest factor a woman desired boiled down to how capable she felt a man was in physically protecting and providing for her and her family. In today's world, this model is obviously outdated; women provide for themselves and are not under constant risk of attack. They primarily need EMOTIONAL SECURITY from a man – someone who keeps his cool while handling not only the challenges of life, but the challenges she brings to him as well.

There is nothing more deeply satisfying for a woman than showing you stay cool under all forms of pressure. Her willingness to confide and trust in you increases exponentially if you have this characteristic in place.

Stop Asking for Permission

This one is huge. Do what YOU want to do. Be a MAN.

I've seen way too many guys make a habit out of saying something that makes me want to slap them. When they're with their wives or girlfriends, some of them have a habit of asking, "Is that all right with you, dear?" As if they need PERMISSION.

This makes me want to vomit. Not because they're being nice and genuinely care about what she wants, but because they have a habit of doing this *constantly*. This usually plays out across every aspect of life – they subordinate to anyone who has influence over them willingly and without question.

The issue lies in the fact that after most guys are born, we never learn how to stop asking for permission. We never learn to break away from the mold society shaped for us from childhood. From birth, we were conditioned repeatedly to obey others or risk punishment. The training began with our parents: we were taught to simply follow their rules. When we grew old enough to start going to school, we were conditioned to follow directions from teachers (otherwise we failed). This process of following directions and doing what we were told stayed with us all the way through our last day of college. Later on after we received a degree and got a job, our habit of obeying our parents and our teachers became our habit of obeying our boss. No matter the age, we were continuously asking for permission throughout each step of the way - from raising our hands to use the bathroom to asking our manager for a few days off of work.

As men, many of us unconsciously carry over this "permission" mindset into marriage. We check to make sure the wife is satisfied with our plans as often as possible, fearing her disapproval and punishment the same way we would our own mother's. Unfortunately, most men have never shifted out of the habit of asking if it's "OK" to do things.

But thinking like this is fatal to your relationships because SOMEONE has to take charge in the relationship. If you're relying on your wife to make all of your decisions, she will start feeling the burden of being both the man and the woman in the marriage. And you can guarantee you will lose 100% of her sexual attraction toward you in the process.

Whether or not you're looking for a wife any time soon (or even enjoy being a bachelor), you have to eliminate the lame habit of asking for permission. Make up your own mind and then take action without worrying what people think. Do what's best for you in the moment by thinking for yourself. This is not an act of selfishness; it's an act of leadership.

Know Where You're Going

Next, know where you're going. Have a plan when you're going on dates for the restaurant you're going to, what you expect her to wear, what activities you've planned afterwards, and your entire agenda in general. Know how to get there and when you're going. Women will begin naturally testing you by taking the reigns once in a while – this is perfectly fine. But if you let a woman do your job for too long, she'll begin losing trust in your capabilities as a man.

The WORST thing you can ever tell a woman on a date if she asks you where you're going to dinner is, "I don't know...wherever you want." This screams lack of confidence and leadership in every possible way. You're basically saying, "I have zero vision and direction." Be the man, be in charge, and play the lead. You're a chump if you don't.

This applies to your entire life as well – know exactly where you're going – what your biggest goals are, and what your most important obligations are to yourself...and go after them with tenacity. I came across a very fitting quote in Sam Keen's book *Fire in The Belly, On Being a Man*:

"There are two questions a man must ask himself. The first is 'Where am I going?' and the second is 'Who will go with me?' If you ever get these questions in the wrong order, you are in trouble."[5]

Figure out the major direction you want to head in life and make no apologies. Your own personal mission must come first before your relationships. If you choose a woman over your purpose in life, you're weakening yourself and becoming less of a man in the process.

Along the way, you're going to have to make some tough decisions (both big and small). Realize that this is a skill that requires you to trust your gut more often than your head. You can certainly utilize your mind to contemplate rational choices, but ultimately you have to trust your instinct enough to just take action. Mistakes will be made, people will be hurt, but you will be better off for it.

This is a hallmark of extremely confident men – they quickly assess a situation, make a gut check, and move forward without hesitation. The more you feel the need to process and analyze the "what-ifs," the weaker your decisions will be. Ask others for help when you need it, but ultimately know that it's YOUR choices that you must make without regret.

Practice making decisions quickly in even the smallest opportunities. When you're in a social setting, tell others where you want to go and what you want to have happen. Adopt the mindset of, "We're going to do this and then we're going to go here." People are universally attracted to certainty and are repulsed by hesitation and indecision. The more firm and decisive you are in your actions, the more compelling you will be with others.

In fact, having strong convictions about certain beliefs or ideas is a highly masculine trait. The more passionate you are about something, the more likely you will take confident actions that are in alignment with what you believe in. Any time you're unsure about a decision, there is a strong likelihood that you don't have clear convictions in that area. Get clear on what's important to you, what you value in life, and stick to it. To truly know where you're going, you need strong beliefs that serve as your unique foundation.

Develop a Killer Instinct

As a man, you need to find the KILLER in you – the guy who will go after his goals without compromise and won't stop until he

41

achieves them. This particular mindset is both necessary in the business world and also extremely appealing to members of the opposite sex. Without the assertive belief in yourself as a true winner and a champion, people won't trust you nearly as much.

Being able to get what you want has massive value. When a girl meets you for the first time, she will intuitively be able to tell if you're the type of guy who gets what he wants. When she thinks about what life would be like with you, she's considering how capable you will be in supporting her. Without this killer instinct, you're not going to be seen as having much value. After all, if you find yourself in a situation where you need to fend for yourself to protect the two of you and you don't know how to get what you want, how could she ever feel truly safe with you?

Here's a big recommendation: as a whole, be more ASSERTIVE. Take action in more spontaneous ways without trying to analyze each scenario first. Be willing to get messy in the process of going after what you want. The less calculated you are in your approach, the more masculine you are. Think ACTION first, then recalculate once tweaks need to be made.

Allow yourself to DOMINATE in areas you excel in. I believe there's a subtle belief in a lot of men that sounds like, "I shouldn't try to act like I'm the best...I should be just good enough to look good. Otherwise, people will think I'm cocky." Take a personal inventory of your best skills and talents. When you perform an activity that you're just naturally brilliant with, don't be afraid to be seen and heard. I'm not telling you to brag about yourself. Instead, behave like you're the BEST. Walk, talk, and act like you're the champion of what you do. This is far more attractive than being shy and hiding your greatest talents. It's OK to kick ass from time to time and wipe with the floor with your competition.

Take Responsibility For Your Life

Most people operate under the illusion that everything in life just happens to them. That they are not in control of the day-to-day events that take place and shape their lives. They believe only what they can see, and this belief is dictated by the assumption that outside forces dominate their realities.

42

This creates a VICTIM mentality. Nothing is ever their fault, nothing is due to their choices, and they cannot be blamed for anything that goes wrong. This warrants a nice and easy escape from responsibility; if nothing is their fault, why should they feel responsible for anything? People that play the victim card usually whine and complain, blaming others and outside powers for all of their problems. They often pity themselves endlessly in an attempt to gain attention from others.

It's so much easier to blame your boss for your misery than to own up to it. It's a lot simpler to lash out at the government, the economy, or a higher power for your own suffering. At the end of the day, if some external reality is responsible for your unhappiness, it means you don't have to be held accountable for your actions.

Here's the deal - a true man doesn't waste his time wallowing in his problems. He recognizes them, develops a strategy for overcoming them, and then takes actions that assume responsibility. He doesn't complain, whine about how tough the circumstances are, or make others into scapegoats.

Realize that complaining is one of the single most unattractive behaviors you could ever take part in. NO ONE appreciates a person complaining or whining. EVER. In fact, people are more interested in how fast it takes paint to dry than listening to all the reasons why life hasn't been fair to you.

So stop whining and accept this one truth, above all others:

You are responsible for every aspect of your life.

If you don't believe this, how could you possibly become confident? How could I possibly help you get to a higher level? If you think the solution lies in areas you can't control, you are helpless. You are choosing to lie face down and get stepped all over.

Here's the big point - you didn't choose when, where, and how you were born. You didn't choose the environment you grew up in. I understand the very beginning of your life was determined by factors outside of your control. I also understand that some are born into better environments than others. These give some an advantage that others don't have.

But this isn't a sociological discussion. We're talking about being the man in the room who demands attention. We're talking about becoming the strongest man you've ever met who is built from the inside-out. To get you there, you must believe that where you are right now is a direct reflection of the choices you've made and continue to make on a daily basis.

This is a make or break point in your journey. By having a firm handle on this idea, you gain an infinitely larger capacity for personal power. And when things go poorly for you, you'll know you have the power to change them. If you shy away from this, most of what you read will be a waste of time.

So take full responsibility for all of your own success and happiness. As a man, depend on no one for your wellbeing. The more you rely on others to take care of you and nurture you, the less in tune you are with your inner confidence. That isn't to say for you to completely ignore support altogether; I believe it's extremely important for you to accept help when others offer it. The key distinction here is to not RELY on it. Don't depend on someone or something outside of you to make things happen. Take the reigns as the leader of your life – you're in the driver seat, you're flying the jet, and you're steering the ship. No one is coming to save you, fix your problems, or correct your mistakes. No one person is going to make life perfect for you. At the end of the day, it's up to you to take full ownership.

So when you make a mistake, OWN it. Don't point the finger in other directions and make excuses for what happened. Openly declare that you've made a mistake, correct it, and see to it that it doesn't happen again. Your willingness to endure pain and frustration without rattling off some lame story about it is a true test of being a man.

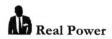 **Real Power**

Desperate. Struggle. Need.

These are three words you need to completely eliminate from your vocabulary. They convey weakness about who you are and what you're capable of. If you're ever desperate, you're telling the world that you yourself cannot survive without something outside of you. If you're struggling, your emotions are too tied up in the process and most of the time, you're not being patient with what you want. If you're in need, you're communicating that you yourself aren't enough. All three of these words ultimately show lack of confidence and conviction in you as a man.

Real power is strictly internal; you have it when you know you have everything you need and that your desire to continue growing and accomplishing more stems from you expressing your talents and abilities, not from a place of lack. You have far more going for you right now than you think – you only need to realize it.

Emotional Weight

You want to think of yourself as ATTRACTING what you want to you – not struggling to PULL it closer to you. The vast majority of people cling to what they want and hysterically claw at it in an attempt to bring it into their lives. Their emotions end up getting tangled up in the process, confusing rational thoughts and blinding their sense of reality. They *emotionally lean* into what they desire, putting their weight onto it, and burdening it with the uncomfortable gravity their longing is creating.

Imagine someone physically leaning on you while you're standing up. A little at first can be comforting; they're seeking your support after all. But imagine this person continuing to lean on you, putting pressure on your balance, forcing more and more of their weight onto you. How do you feel at this point? What's going to happen to both of you? Depending on how much you like the person, you'll either fall over together or you'll throw them off you to regain your stance. Either way, you're not too happy this person has taken away your balance in order to support their own.

45

When you depend on someone else for your own peace of mind, you are leaning on him or her for support. Whether you think it's obvious or not, both of you know this subconsciously at all times. During the beginning of your relationship, you might be giving the person an ego boost as they realize they can directly influence your own happiness. Over time, however, this quickly becomes annoying and exhausting.

You never need to seek approval from others. This is akin to showing your hand in a game of poker - all of the mystery and curiosity in who you are and what you're bringing to the table vanishes when you seek approval. You're telegraphing, "I need you people to like me so I can feel safe here." Be wary of doing or saying things simply to just get noticed. You don't need to "act cool" or show off for people to like you – if you're truly a cool guy, people will find out on their own.

When you try to build rapport with someone else in a way that seems forced or desperate, you drown out all possible connection with your own self-doubt. You remind that person of his or her own insecurities, and as a result, they feel repulsed by you. You're sucking the energy out of the room and leaching it off of others.

This brings up an important point - if you want to be accepted by others, accept yourself first. If you want to be acknowledged and feel like you have the right to belong, acknowledge yourself first. You are the only person who can give you permission to be cool and likeable. No one can ever grant you that feeling. So stop looking for others to hand it to you and stand on your own two feet. Understand that no one can ever let you down if you're not leaning against them.

The Power of Tension

Whether you're looking to go on higher quality dates with women, get more sales and earn more money, negotiate more successfully, or strengthen your overall demeanor, understanding and applying this key concept will make a huge difference. This is something most men are absolutely clueless about.

Imagine two people working toward a common goal that lies in the middle between them. Picture a cord attached to both of them that gets taut when one or both pulls away and slack when they come together.

As both move toward the goal, their desire for obtaining it increases. This is because the more work and effort we invest into something, the more we want to have it. What takes time and energy to obtain is almost always met with outstretched arms. However, what comes easily to us is often unappreciated, under-valued, or even forgotten once we receive it.

With this in mind, picture yourself as a typical guy on a date with a woman you find extremely attractive. As soon as you meet her, her beauty strikes you as rare and compelling; you don't have many opportunities to meet women like this. You believe you're going to have to work hard to fully capture her attention. So what do you do? You shower her with gifts, pay for everything you do together, and assume everything about her will fit perfectly into your life. Subconsciously, you're terrified that you will screw up this rare opportunity and be left alone again.

Here's what that situation looks like:

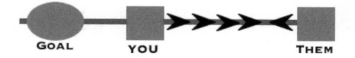

Because all of your emotional weight is leaning heavily on a potential romance, it becomes immediately clear to her that she will not have to put much effort into meeting you halfway for a relationship. The game you're playing (the date) becomes boring to her because it's too easy to win – there's no challenge left. As a result, there's no desire for her to continue seeing you or taking you seriously. At this point, the best-case scenario for you is for her to totally ignore you and move on. Otherwise, she may very well try to use you for your credit card to score free meals and clothes while she romantically pursues another man.

What men like these need to understand is this: there can't be ATTRACTION without TENSION. As two people move closer to a goal, they experience desire. However, if one pulls *away* from a goal (even slightly), the other experiences tension. This feeling of tension then naturally leads that person to move closer. Ironically, it's the very thing necessary to create a recipe of attraction.

In Oren Klaff's book, *Pitch Anything*, the author keenly breaks down what makes business pitches successful. He explains that there are three facts about human beings that hasn't changed since the dawn of mankind:

1. We chase that which moves away from us

2. We want what we cannot have

3. We only place value on things that are difficult to obtain[6]

These three facts can be applied to any situation where someone else is judging who you are and what you have going for you. The key isn't to simply work hard to show the other side how valuable you are or how great your idea is. The key is to ramp up their desire by adding tension to your moments together. When you do this, you make yourself more valuable, sought after, rare, and difficult to win over.

You can accomplish this in several different ways:

You can ask the person to qualify him/herself to you: "Can you tell me more about yourself? What makes you special/unique/different/etc.?"

You can poke fun at small mistakes they make: "I don't know if you're ready for prime time yet, rookie..."

You can send mixed signals: "You know what? We're just not a good fit together." Then smile and kiss her cheek.

You can let some time go by before you contact someone again (or answer a call) after they last spoke with you.

You can withdraw at a moment where they would expect you to pursue. If you're talking on the phone, say, "I think I've figured out something about you no one has ever told you before..." When they respond with, "What?!" Simply say, "I'll have to tell you tomorrow – it's getting late." Making yourself scarce always keeps tension alive.

You can take someone apologizing to you for something small and exaggerate it. For example, if a server tells you, "I hope you don't mind I just split your bill down the middle," you can say jokingly, "Ohhhh now you've ruined the entire meal. This is just *great*. Where is your manager?"

Be careful in using some of these techniques if you're going to come off harsh and cold; you want to leave room for someone to think you might be kidding or not taking it too seriously. The best tension is usually laced with humor – in fact, there is no situation where humor doesn't add to the experience – as long as it's used with class and you're not forcing it too heavily. As an added bonus, if someone else is laughing at what you're saying and seems to be having a good time, you are getting a nice two-for-one deal: they enjoy being around you AND want to have you around more often.

Keep in mind that if you apply TOO much tension, the other person will probably lose interest altogether because they will believe the goal is too difficult to achieve. Just remember this simple idea: when the game becomes too easy, it gets boring. When it gets too challenging, it gets frustrating. Strike the perfect blend right in the middle and you'll be just fine.

Salvaging a Broken Heart

If a friendship doesn't end well or a relationship falls apart, don't chase after the person. You've probably seen far too many romantic comedies with the main character chasing his lost lover through an airport, catching up to her before she boards her flight, and convincing her to stay and fall back in love with him. As romantic as this is, behaving like this doesn't translate well in reality. When you chase after someone who left you, you're completely devaluing yourself. No matter how much you believe you were "meant to be together," there is a definite reason why the relationship ended. Respect that and learn to give it space.

Men that truly value themselves move on when things don't work out with another person. They intuitively know that any actions they might take from a place of desperation will almost always fall short. During this time, his energy is all over the place, his emotions are twisted up, and clinging to someone who doesn't love him anymore clouds his vision.

Your best option (if you in fact do want to attract the person back into your life) is to cut off all communication with her and dig deeper into what excites you, challenges you, and teaches you. Instead of wallowing in self-pity with the lights off under the bed sheets, do things that inspire you. Release the emotions from the relationship and be strong enough to sit in silence. By raising your energy and growing throughout the process, if and when she does come back to you, you will be coming from a place of strength and not weakness. She will begin to wonder what she is missing, and the cycle of desire and tension can begin again.

You can thank Jerry Maguire for the whole "you complete me" cliché about relationships. As if half of you is missing until you find that special somebody. Here's a better idea: *if you genuinely feel like you can't function without another person in your life, your heart was broken to begin with.* You never believed you were worthy and deserving of happiness on your own and sought fulfillment in others. From now on, eliminate this weak belief and take this one to heart:

No one ever "completes" you. They *meet* you.

When you meet someone without feeling like part of you is yearning for what's missing, you see one another eye to eye. She doesn't become the solution to your problems. She doesn't become your one and only source of bliss. She doesn't become your salvation. If the relationship ends, you have lost NOTHING. You have simply gained new experiences, memories, and discoveries along the way.

Don't throw your emotional weight around - keep it centered within you at all times. Look to yourself for your own happiness and strength. No one and nothing else can give you that. You are enough.

 Be a Man of Value

When you come from a place of inner-happiness, you know that your own approval, focus, strength, and joy give you everything you need to survive. As a result, every person you come into contact with, every relationship you have, and every business opportunity that comes up is a chance for you to share your value without attachment.

The more time, energy, and effort you devote to consistently growing and improving yourself, the more others will be irresistibly drawn to you. People will always invest in you if you invest in yourself and people will always value you when you value yourself.

This is about you being an amazing and confident guy with no strings attached.

Devote Time to Improve Yourself

Open a book and download as much valuable knowledge into your brain as you can. Learn a new language. Master a new skill or art form. Take an online class. Travel to a new country and take home part of the culture. Do something new you can teach someone else. The more valuable information you continuously dump into your mind, the more valuable you become to others.

The beauty of choosing to do this instead of wasting away in front of your television is because when you GIVE yourself insightful knowledge and information, you will naturally want to GIVE it to others. Your conversations have a higher chance of impacting someone and making him or her want to be around you more

51

often. You become infinitely more interesting and you stand out from every other boring guy they run into.

Remember that the more work and effort we put into something, the more we tend to respect and appreciate it. If you're looking for a really easy and straightforward way to feel better about yourself, enhance your creativity, knowledge, skills, talents, and habits so others more easily recognize them. After all, the definition of appreciation is to increase the value of something. Giving yourself more reasons to appreciate you will only position you as a more attractive commodity.

Treat Yourself Like a Precious Diamond

Inside every man is a genius that is yearning for its full expression. Feed it by spending time doing what you love the most and whatever gives you the most fulfillment. If you recognize its existence no matter how "stupid" or "uninspired" you think you are, you have the potential to affect thousands of lives. Your conviction in this skyrockets your confidence immensely.

As you're building inner value, cultivate your outer image as well. Wear clothes you feel crisp, sharp, and powerful in. Take care of your appearance – shave, cut your nails, keep your hair maintained, and take care of your body. Unshakable Swagger isn't dictated solely by what you wear or the conditioner you prefer, but understand that what you put on has a powerful impact on your state of mind. You can't tell me you feel the same in a pair of sweat pants as opposed to a suit.

Keep this in mind: what you look like really doesn't matter but how you arrange your style communicates how highly you think of yourself (and this is extremely important). If you want to be another John in a sea of Johns, choose to present yourself in a way that says, "I just threw this on because it doesn't matter." Subconsciously, what you're really saying is, "I don't matter." You need to treat yourself like a RARE and PRECIOUS diamond. Focus on how your special skills and knowledge makes you unique and then decide on the most effective way to transmit that message to the universe. Don't hide and play small by blending in or haphazardly selecting your wardrobe. Let your genius be seen clearly and precisely.

Also, keep a clean and tidy environment around you. Being sloppy with your living and working situation is another way of saying you don't deserve the best in your life. If you're too lazy about cleaning the space around you, hire a maid. The space you both live and work in has a direct effect on how you think about yourself. If you're surrounded by disarray, your thoughts will naturally be chaotic, scattered, and unfocused. If you take care of your environment, you will feel more in control, organized, and happier with yourself. Remove all the clutter and junk you don't need anymore so you're not negatively affected.

Lastly, give yourself room to make mistakes. Don't ever beat yourself up for your failures and miscues. Take the lesson from your experience and get back to work. If you give yourself total love and acceptance, you will never stress or worry about important moments in your life. You will always have a base line to come back to, even if things go horribly wrong. It can be easy to forget this, so I suggest printing off a huge poster that says something like, "PERMISSION TO SCREW UP."

More often than not, our greatest enemy is ourself. We tend to abuse ourselves when things don't go our way and we slip up. How many times have you caught yourself saying something like, "You idiot! What were you thinking?!" Every time you do this, you're damaging your self-esteem and cutting down the very confidence you say you want to build. The key is to give yourself unconditional love and support – even when you make grave mistakes. You must take a stand with protecting the psyche of the person that matters most in your life – you.

 Push Your Comfort Zone

What comes to mind when you think of today's rites of passage for manhood? Going through a Bar Mitzvah? Landing a part-time job? Getting into a fistfight? Having your first sexual encounter?

53

Driving your own car? Graduating college? There's a combination of events guys experience throughout the teenage years and early twenties that have a big impact on what society tells us is important in becoming a man. Yet nothing definitively proves we have become men or stands alone as the big passage into adulthood.

One of the things we lost in progressing as a species was a specific ritual into adulthood. Sam Keen describes the tough and often brutal rites of passage for pre-modern societies in his book, *Fire in the Belly: On Being a Man.* While every community designed this process differently, almost every ritual enforced a separation of the boys from all females in the group. They were isolated for a period of time away from the warmth and protection of their mothers and sent to an all-male gathering to learn how to become warriors. The boys' bodies were beaten and often mutilated. Food was often forgotten altogether. Only when the elders felt that the boys had become capable of protecting the community would they be released back to the group. Every single boy knew unquestionably that he had become a warrior, a protector, and a MAN.

The boys of this time were actually given permission to assume power. In becoming an adult, they were given new responsibilities and acknowledged for their transformation. Without this clear awareness of empowerment, our ancestors doubted their offspring would possess the necessary confidence to handle the duties of protecting the tribe.[7]

Fast forward to today. While war is still very real, we are blessed with not having to defend our country if we don't choose to. The boys today prepare for war by murdering millions of digitally simulated soldiers from the comfort of their couches. We have clearly advanced well beyond the way things used to be thousands of years ago. I am immensely grateful to live in a world where I am not required to kill another human being in order to survive. But living in a world so safe and comfortable has domesticated far too many of us. With no threat of DANGER to be found, we can't put what it takes to be a man to the test. We can't become ALIVE.

Now you might come from an environment where the threat of death was a very real thing. I don't mean to offend anyone or insinuate that everyone is "safe" or "protected" in today's world.

I'm speaking to the vast majority of guys reading this book. You know who you are - those of us who weren't physically and mentally pushed to a breaking point. How do *we* prove that we're men?

Choose to Push Your Limits

I suggest you make it a voluntary choice - an ongoing decision to discipline your fear and reach into the unknown, away from the comforts of the familiar and safe. Each step outside of your comfort zone will stretch your limits and tolerance for fear, pain, and danger. Because when you are in a perpetually comfortable environment, understanding who you are and what you are made of becomes impossible.

Any time you're uncomfortable, you're forced to grow and adapt. This process of putting pressure on yourself demands that you learn to trust yourself on a CORE level. When your environment changes and you're facing a new situation that is completely unknown to you, you evolve and become capable of taking on more. Your blueprint expands and your identity grows larger. During these moments, you learn to give yourself permission to be powerful and to summon up courage lying dormant.

Conversely, if you maintain a habit of staying comfortable and seeking security, even tiny obstacles can be brick walls to your progress. Helen Keller possesses one of my favorite quotes on the illusion of security: "Security is mostly a superstition. It does not exist in nature, nor do the children of men as a whole experience it. Avoiding danger is no safer in the long run than outright exposure. Life is either a daring adventure, or nothing."

I urge you to be a player in the game – to get messy, dive in with both feet, and embrace new experiences that stretch you as a man. Don't sit on the sidelines as a spectator, watching other people live out their dreams on television. If you're afraid of making mistakes, getting hurt, or failing, I got news for you: it's unavoidable. You're going to screw up, get physically and emotionally bruised, and face defeat throughout your life. Rather than trying to avoid these things, accept their inevitability.

Your business partners, closest friends, and lovers won't trust you at a deep and necessary level if you relax through life on cruise control. They won't be able to look you in the eyes and know you're in control if chaos arrives unexpectedly. Do you think a General would retain his position for even a second if it were obvious he wasn't accustomed to dealing with the unfamiliar?

There are a variety of ways you can stretch your limits – you can master discipline by practicing martial arts, face your fear of performance anxiety by taking improvisation classes or acting in local theater, risk rejection by approaching a beautiful woman and asking her out on a date, or conquering your fear of heights by skydiving. If you're not sure about what you'd like to do, ask yourself, "What am I truly afraid of?" and do what scares you. Commit to that action, ask a few friends to either do it with you or hold you accountable, and follow through on it. The accompanying exhilaration you feel after expanding your comfort zone is endlessly rewarding.

Here's my big disclaimer: when you attempt something new for the first time, especially something you are fearful of, your conditioned mind is going to do anything it can to stop you from moving forward. As soon as you encounter some pain from taking action, whether it's the icy cold wind hitting your face from being seventeen thousand feet in the air or the uncomfortable stare you receive from a woman shooting you down in public, you will have an instinctive response to retreat back to your comfort zone immediately. You will know exactly when this occurs because you'll catch yourself thinking, "Screw this!"

Each time you retreat, the next time you try to move forward, you will feel additional pain and suffering. If you can overcome your conditioned mind screaming at you to return to your comfort zone and simply stay the course, you will eventually be able to completely follow through on your fears. So rather than repeatedly starting and stopping, commit to totally IMMERSING yourself in your fears, refusing to back away from them until you have reached a higher level of confidence. This not only allows the process of expanding your comfort zone to be less painful, it ensures you make steady and consistent progress.

Integrity

Having integrity means your values match up with your behaviors. It is you fulfilling what you said you would do, especially if it is important to you and/or someone else. This is what makes people trust you more than anything else. When your thoughts and beliefs are congruent with how you're showing up in life, you are living with integrity.

However, when you go against your word, flake on an appointment, or make excuses for something not getting done, your level of respect plummets immensely. The most important person offended by your lack of integrity is not the other party. It's actually YOU. Although you may think that temporary feeling of guilt will pass and be replaced by something else, your true self knows better.

Our culture as a whole doesn't truly value integrity; most of the time when we hear the word come up, we just think it means "honesty." However, being honest is only half of the equation. The other, more neglected half comes from doing what you said you were going to do *even when you don't feel like it*. This doesn't interest most of our society because most people believe a valid excuse for not following through on a commitment is: "I didn't feel like doing it."

There is a HUGE PROBLEM with allowing this excuse to permeate your life: the only way to ensure that you become unstoppably confident and able to fully trust yourself is to ALWAYS KEEP YOUR WORD. Otherwise, the belief you have in yourself will be flimsy at best.

> **DO WHAT YOU SAID YOU WERE GOING TO DO EVEN WHEN YOU DON'T FEEL LIKE IT**

You may think that telling yourself you will wake up early and hit the gym, then snoozing through your alarm clock and saying, "Oh I'll just do it tomorrow" isn't a big deal. But EVERYTHING in the world of integrity is a BIG DEAL. Because the next time you make a commitment or set a goal you want to achieve, your mind will think, "Yeah, but you didn't follow through on this last time – why would this time be any different?" This subconscious belief will rob your feelings of power and worthiness faster than anything else can.

If you want to take advantage of the fastest method of gaining self-confidence, keep your word when no one else is watching and refuse to ever let your emotions become an excuse for not following through. Practice integrity when you are the only person who knows whether or not you keep your word. This isn't about showing off to other people – this is about you strengthening your character and increasing your self-respect.

If you were to ask me to give you the top ten ways to increase confidence, I would rank keeping your word in the top five – if not number one. The more you keep your word, the more you believe in your ability to create what you want in your life. When you declare, "I'm going to go to the gym three times a week until I lose twenty pounds," you inherently trust in yourself to do it. No matter how much failure you have piled up in the past, having integrity gives you the power to believe you can achieve anything.

So follow through on everything you talk about. When you speak about what matters to you and the values you want to share with the world, it's not about merely talking about them - philosophizing and rambling on about them - it's about showing them with your actions. Ever heard the expression "walk the walk?" This is where you apply it. Stop mouthing off about how many things you are going to achieve in your life unless you are committed to taking action with them. From this moment forward, don't say you are going to do something unless you are 100% sure you will follow through.

To help you keep your word, increase your accountability. Hire a coach or personal trainer who will keep your feet to the fire and hold you accountable for doing what you say you're going to do.

Having someone like this in your life ensures that you value integrity and won't let you go against your word. If you don't have the funds available, keep a journal, write down your goals, and log exactly how much effort you're putting toward them every day. Numbers don't lie, especially when they're holding you aCOUNTable. Putting them in front of you every day keeps your weak areas in plain sight and pushes you toward improvement.

Lastly, hold yourself to a higher standard - not compared to what other people are doing, but to your own expectations. Continuously work to raise your game and aim for daunting goals. Every man should be growing each year, accepting more responsibility and living into his passion. Those unwilling to grow will be nagged by their wives or girlfriends and ultimately rejected in favor of a guy willing to expand and demand more from life. If you're in a relationship, you should be open to your significant other both supporting you and holding you accountable to what you say you want. Hold yourself to a standard of ever-increasing excellence.

If you keep your actions in alignment with your words, you have honor. You are precisely the man who is ready to begin fine-tuning his skills in communication to project Unshakable Swagger to the world around you. If you take these foundational principles to heart and begin implementing them into your life, what you're about to read will be easier and more intuitive.

Because we just covered a lot of information in just a few pages, review this chapter as often as possible to really lock the concepts into place. Whenever you feel thrown off course, I suggest returning to these first few chapters and re-reading these concepts.

Onto part two...

PART TWO:
THE SWAGGER

Build your life on the strongest
foundation possible.

4

BODY LANGUAGE
FLUENCY

"I speak two languages – Body and English." – Mae
West

Now that we've established a stronger structure to build on, let's move onto more of the specifics: how to move, talk, behave, and think to project confidence. I'm kicking this part of the book off with body language because it is critical to master this area first. Poor body language can be so damaging to your confidence that even if you are full of creative ideas and usually have something clever to say, it can get you ignored completely. You can be the next Gandhi, but if you're hunched over, fidgeting constantly, and unable to look anyone in the eyes, it really won't matter.

Every time I have a conversation with a client who wants to feel more confident, almost 100% of the time, they ask for what to say in specific circumstances. I explain to them that while knowing "what to say" is helpful, it pales in comparison to strong body language. In fact, the vast majority of the time, you can pretty much say whatever you want to as long as you're not boring or offending someone. This is often completely overlooked when we're thinking about the words we want to speak, and yet it dominates all forms of communication.

If you incorporate these changes into your life, I guarantee you will see others responding to you in a completely new light. With time, you can then notice all of the subconscious gestures others show and think are private to themselves. As you open up your perceptions, you will eventually gain the ability to completely shift focus off of yourself and read those around you. You can adapt to what their body language is telling you and make friends faster, network more efficiently, and land a higher quality of dates. These are some of the benefits of becoming fluent in this type of communication.

Here's what you're about to learn:

- Why this type of communication is more powerful than words

- How to move your body to convey charisma and strength

- How to develop strong eye contact and a killer smile

- Easy body language mistakes to avoid

 Body Language is Hard-Wired

Before our species ever had a spoken language, we used expressions, gestures, and read clues about one another's behaviors to determine what another person was feeling. Back in the caveman era, there wasn't anyone saying, "There's a huge animal with sharp teeth on its way, we better get the hell out of here!" To cope with this, humans read wide eyes, raised eyebrows, and an open mouth to indicate fear and the need to move quickly. Your subconscious mind has never forgotten the first way we shared thoughts between one another. This is communication at its most primal level.

Because it's hard-wired into our species, it is much more powerful than the words we use to express ourselves. Albert Mehrabian's famous Psychology Today article states that in many situations, only 7% of our communication is verbal while 93% is facial or body expression and tone of voice.[8]

Let that sink in for a minute.

Our spoken language determines only SEVEN PERCENT of communication. Can you see how thinking about what to say isn't really that big of a deal?

Your body language comes mostly from your subconscious mind, which is why you're usually unaware of what you're doing. Your mind takes your most frequent thoughts and beliefs and literally projects them through your body. When you're feeling awkward or holding a lot of tension in your mind, the outer world sees this written all over you. Conversely, when you're thinking strong, positive thoughts, you communicate them easily with powerful body language.

So if you ever feel out of place somewhere, stop thinking about what you're going to say and dial it back to your physiology. Here's a quick tip: as you change your posture, your motion, your expressions, and your amount of eye contact, you change how you feel. This is known as the Facial Feedback Hypothesis. It's effective because your brain takes in clues from your physiology and then dictates the emotions you will experience. If you are feeling anxious or worried in a specific situation, literally holding your shoulders back, chest up, smiling, and taking a wider stance with your feet will make you feel more comfortable.

If you have a strong handle on body language, you can communicate several powerful messages about who you are in nanoseconds. Some of them include your status, independence, how comfortable you are in your own skin, how well you treat yourself, your peace of mind, and how trustworthy you are.

However, if you have *poor* body language, you communicate several damning messages about who are just as quickly such as: neediness, weakness, being scattered and unfocused, poor self-esteem, and a lack of social skills.

Your physiology is the most efficient method of communication you have. Recognize that the people you're speaking to are receiving a message on two levels: the CONTENT of your verbal language and the CONTEXT of your body language. You can compare the impact of the speed of your words to a horse and carriage and the impact of the speed of your physicality to a McLaren MP4-28. By the time a person has understood what you've spoken, they've already formed hundreds of observations based on how you've said it. In other words, your body language is YELLING while your spoken words are WHISPERING.

 Mastering Movement

The way you walk tells a lot about what you have going for you. If you shuffle your feet, hang your head, and slump your shoulders while you walk at a snail's pace, it becomes immediately clear there's not a whole lot going on in your world. Remember, your confidence mirrors how you arrange your body; start walking with conviction and you will automatically start feeling more confident - even if you're not going anywhere special.

So any time you're walking from one point to another, do so with PURPOSE. Don't hesitate, flounder around, or lackadaisically wander. Make a firm decision about where you're going and walk like you mean it. You want to make it a habit to move like you have things to do and no time to waste.

When you're taking strides, let your arms sway naturally when you walk. Not enough makes you look like a robot. Too much makes you look, well dainty. Watch John Travolta "strut" in *Saturday Night Fever* to get a good idea of what I'm talking about. He takes long relaxed strides with a slight bounce in his step, rocking gently from side to side as he moves. He lets his arms swing comfortably out in front of him without looking mechanical. Do this.

As you start getting the hang of it, think about where your core strength comes from. You don't want to lead with your head or your chest out in front; you want your core leading the way. To do this, lead with your waist when you walk. Pretend you have a string tied around your hips pulling you wherever you're going. Suck in your gut and rock your shoulders back and allow your hips to guide you.

As a whole, slow down all of your movements. Quick, spastic motions typically convey anxiousness. Slow down your walk, the way you turn your head, how you reach for things, and the gestures you use when speaking. You'll notice you feel more in control of your body and your surroundings. You want your motions to be calculated and done without hesitation. When you do something, MEAN it and don't waste your energy.

If you want to get someone's attention, call him or her over to you instead of chasing them down. Know where you're going and pull people into your vicinity by asking them to join you where you stand. You want to LEAD with your movement, not follow. By following others to get their attention, you're subtly leaning into their acceptance of you.

A really cool tip to keep in mind is that whoever stands in the middle of a group comes across as the leader of the group subconsciously. Conversely, whoever stands on the outside of the group comes across as the follower. This applies to even small groups of three or four. If you want to be more active in conversations, be sure to stand with people on both sides of you instead of leaning in from the outside. Again, this subtlety between moving towards people verses attracting them into your reality is huge.

In general, make confident movements on your own without looking to see if others are doing the same. For example, if you're about to cross a busy street, don't wait for those around you to walk first. Take the first step and LEAD them. Do what you want to do more often without checking to see if it's "OK" or "SAFE." We have an innate tendency to first look for feedback from those close to us before we take action – it's a well-known phenomenon called Social Proof. However, people will always follow a man who knows where he's going in spite of the behavior of those in his environment. In order to care what people think about you less often, eliminate any dependence on their conduct as a model for your actions.

 Strong Posture

Having strong posture means more than just keeping your back straight and holding your shoulders back. You want to also suck in your gut and push your chest out to open yourself up. If you hunch your back and round your shoulders forward, not only do you look weak, but you also look defensive an uninviting. Want to hear a fun fact? A person can easily figure out who the leader of a group of primates is by observing how open and wide its body language is. Humans are no different; by standing up and making yourself physically bigger, you convey power and dominance.

Your head is the key component of firm posture. According to social psychologist Amy Cuddy's demonstration at her Ted Talks Presentation, holding your head back at a slight tilt conveys the universal expression of pride – a person who feels victorious and happy. Conversely, letting your head hang down with your neck jutting forward doesn't just make you look like a turtle – it projects weakness and inferiority. Simply holding your head back makes a tremendous difference in both the message you portray and how you feel about yourself.[9]

When you stand, your overall composure should be relaxed but firm. Distribute your weight evenly between your feet to stay balanced. Keep your feet slightly more than shoulder width apart and don't be afraid to take up space. If you're too closed off, you won't have a steady stature and you can be pushed over easily. You want to be a ROCK.

In general, lean back when you're talking to people, especially women. If you lean in towards a woman, you're telegraphing interest in her and showing your poker hand too early. When you lean in, you take up someone else's space and their natural reaction is to back away from you. Instead, lean back and invite people to come closer to you to talk. This applies especially to loud environments where listening becomes difficult. If someone has to lean in closer to hear, let the other person be the one to do it. And under *no circumstances* should you ever bend down to hear someone; your slouching posture is both effeminate and weak.

When you're sitting down, keep your feet wide and lay an arm across the seat back occasionally. When you're standing up, lean against your environment by putting a foot up against the wall. "Marking your territory" like this is primal and rooted in strong masculinity. This will assist you in warding off attempts at intimidation; the more secure you feel, the more confident you are.

You can utilize the Facial Feedback hypothesis to your advantage with your posture. Before a job interview, public speech, performance, or any other crucial event, practice strong body posture for a few minutes at a time – tilt your head back, hold your shoulders back, and open up your physiology. Think of this as "priming" yourself for confident body language beforehand. Your confidence will actually increase dramatically because your emotions will match the context of what your body is doing.

Remember that your overall posture serves as the container you present your inner beliefs and thoughts in. If the container appears weak, the inner contents probably aren't being protected or reinforced - meaning mental frailties are likely to rear their ugly head. Flex a strong posture and people will instantly believe one important thing about you: "This guy really has himself put together."

 Bold Eye Contact

Eye contact is the ULTIMATE communication tool you need to understand how to properly utilize. When you fail to look someone in the eyes when you're speaking to them, a couple of things are going to run through their head: you're not listening, you're distracted by something, or you're too self-conscious. Again, this is yet another example of how what you say can fall apart thanks to how you're saying it. If you don't cultivate the habit of making eye contact, your insecurities and inability to concentrate will (unfortunately) be readily apparent.

This is because your eyes are always betraying the thoughts you think are private during a conversation. Human beings intuitively study one another's eyes to see if there is congruence between our words and our innermost thoughts. That's why it is difficult to believe someone is telling the truth when their gaze is going wildly across the room. People flat-out will not trust you unless they can get a sense of a stable optic connection. In fact, Hemsley and Doob's research (1978) points out that frequent eye contact shows intimacy and the proper amount of respect – both of which lead to an increase in trust.[10] It is said that the eyes are the window to the soul, after all.

So make sure to maintain solid eye contact with everyone you speak to. Don't look down, don't look around sporadically, and *especially* don't stare at a woman's chest. If you're looking down and away when you're talking, what you're really expressing is, "Don't pay too much attention to me; what I say doesn't really matter that much."

How long you maintain eye contact is vital to confident body language and whether or not you can be taken seriously. When you first meet someone, don't be the first person to look away unless you want to appear less dominant (like around your fiancé's father). This is a BIG one with the ladies. If you lock eyes with a woman for the first time and immediately look away, you've already dropped the ball. Conversely, if you lock eyes and hold your gaze until *she* breaks it, you will ratchet up her attraction to you quickly.

The key to this whole aspect of body language is to have warm, welcoming eyes with a slight smirk on your face. If you bore into someone's pupils with a demented stare, you're just going to be seen as a creep. Likewise, don't hold eye contact throughout the *entire* interaction because you're probably going to come across as a serial killer. As with anything, balance is best.

If you find yourself struggling, stand in front of a mirror and lock eyes for a few minutes every day until you get more comfortable. Alternate between focusing on both eyes at the same time and then one individually. Then practice increasing eye contact with your friends and family at first, then the people who ring you up at the grocery store, and then to take it to the next level, lock eyes with each woman you walk by until they look away before you. This process will feel slightly like staring directly into the sun, but don't let the initial discomfort stop you from mastering it.

Because it can be difficult at first to get into this habit if you're not accustomed to it, try this exercise. Sit face to face with someone you know well enough to trust you. Grab your cell phone and set the timer on it to sixty seconds. Look directly into one another's eyes without talking, laughing, or breaking eye contact. Be sure to pay careful attention to how much resistance you feel during the exercise. Anytime one of you laughs or looks away, restart from zero. As you complete this a few times, you'll start feeling more comfortable holding eye contact and overcoming the urge to look away.

Ultimately seek to practice this as often as you can. The next time you're on a date with a woman, try looking into her eyes without saying anything. Most guys are terrified of silence like this and would rather stick their finger into an electric socket. Don't be intimidated. Your ability to hold rock steady eye contact even in potentially awkward moments like this will make you a stronger man. You absolutely cannot have style or swagger if you fall short in this department.

 The Science of Smiling

You've probably read about smiling in every single 'How Do I Be More Confident' article or book ever written in the history of time. Yes, you should smile. I realize this isn't exactly new information.

The key is how you smile and how often you smile. There's a huge difference between smiling in an attempt to make people like you

71

and smiling out of your own amusement. You want to smile regardless of whether or not someone else is smiling along with you. The look on your face should be, "I don't care if you find this amusing. I do."

Grinning like this adds an air of mystery to your personality. People will begin wondering, "What is going on? Why's he smiling like that? What's so funny?" To quote Herman Melville, "a smile is the chosen vehicle for all ambiguity." Here's a fun experiment: during a quiet moment between you and a date, flash a big smile and laugh a little to yourself without explaining it. When she asks about it, simply reply, "oh nothing." Raising questions with your body language without answering them is like lighting dynamite and refusing to put out the fuse. You will drive people crazy!

You want to flash the smile and hold it briefly - don't keep it plastered on your face like a used car salesman. Experiment with twisting it into a slight smirk: a wry grin with a hint of cockiness. If you're flirting with someone and want to take the conversation from a friendly level to a flirtatious level, throw in a few of these wry smiles and you'll be seen as charming. This works just about every time and ensures you have a fun and playful night together.

Also, as a side note, I just don't get why a lot of guys take on the "tough guy" approach out in public and choose to never smile or laugh. What they don't realize is that not only are they NOT coming across as 007, they're making it seem like they're REALLY not having a good time. The more you smile and laugh around others, the more people see you as a source of good feelings and ultimately isn't that what you want? Being overly stoic and stone-faced will not motivate others to connect with you.

 Your Hands

The hands are the easiest part of the body to locate nervousness. If you're fidgeting with something or making spastic gestures with them, it's impossible for you to look comfortable. If you don't know what to do with your hands, put them in your back pockets until you make it a habit of keeping them by your side. Even if you're not nervous very often, you need to eliminate anxious gestures from your life entirely.

Oh, and stop touching yourself.

A common coping mechanism for people dealing with anxiety tends to show up through self-touch in an effort to comfort oneself. The most famous example of this is Nixon during the Watergate Hearings. As he's defending himself at the podium, he holds his hands behind his back and unconsciously rubs them together, as if to say, "It's okay, Richard, we're going to get through this." When you watch the tape of the hearing, you immediately see him fidgeting with his hands like this and it becomes obvious he doesn't feel very confident.

With that being said, don't rub your neck, bite your fingernails, fidget with your hair, or repeatedly touch any part of your body. These behaviors make you look defensive and communicating defensiveness is never a good recipe for composure. Most of the time when we commit these mistakes, we do them unconsciously, so it may be helpful to have a friend watch you for a few hours and let you know if and when you do these things.

On the flip side, you should feel comfortable putting your hands on others (in appropriate ways of course). Placing a hand on someone's shoulder conveys trust and subtly shows dominance. Use this to get someone's attention when you want to show yourself as a social leader. Another subtle technique is to guide someone where you want them to go by putting your hand on his or her back. When you guide someone through a doorway in front of you and then walk in behind them, you're acting as the host of the situation. While this is subtle in Western culture, it's actually a huge deal in Middle Eastern culture – the most authoritative male always walks through a doorway last.

In the dating world, physical contact is critical to smoothly transitioning into a sexual relationship. The longer you wait to make a physical connection after meeting a woman, the more awkward she'll feel when you try to make a move. This is why it is always a terrible idea to spend an entire date with someone only to wait until saying goodbye to go for the first kiss. Touching her forearms, shoulders, and hands throughout the date establish a comfortable pattern for the two of you. Give her high-fives, brush something off her shirt, thumb wrestle, give her a few hugs, grab her knee, playfully shove her when you're walking together, and look to hold hands with her before you go for the first kiss. Just don't be weird by keeping your hands on her for an extended period of time.

You don't have to feel like you don't have the right to make physical contact with people. Most are comfortable with it and depending on how likeable you are, will prefer it as long as you respect their space. The worst thing in the world is to come down with a case of "hover hands." Google it if you have no idea what I'm talking about.[11]

If someone invades your space accidentally or bumps into you, stop saying, "sorry" unconsciously. On the flip side, if you bump into someone, of course you need to apologize, but erase the lame habit of apologizing when someone else does it altogether. Stop making it clear you're unaccustomed to coming across new people. If a member of the opposite sex ever bumps into you, make a joke out of it. "Oh so *this* is how you meet new guys?" Don't escape from the situation with a lame apology.

Lastly, you need to have a STRONG handshake and look someone in the eyes when you meet them. If you're meeting an alpha male who's clearly squeezing a little too hard, point your index finger (like you're forming a gun) and your hand will immediately strengthen. Try it sometime; it's a nice trick I picked up. You can also simply put your other hand on top of theirs to give the guy a "hand hug" so you maintain control.

 ## The Belly Button Rule

Janine Driver coined the Belly Button Rule in her book *You Say More Than You Think*. There is an enormous psychological difference between standing close to someone and pointing your whole body at them and standing close to someone and pointing away from them. The Belly Button Rule refers to the direction your belly button is facing and how you need to be mindful of the messages you and other people send with it.[12]

You can tell which person someone is truly paying attention to based on the direction of his or her belly button. This is useful information to know when you're speaking in front of a group – formally or casually. If people are facing you with their entire bodies, you're doing a solid job holding their attention. However, if they aren't, you need to make some adjustments to retain their focus. If you're in a situation where you're competing for a girl's attention with other guys, the direction her body is facing shows who she's truly interested in the most.

Speaking of the ladies, this rule is important to master if you prefer going out to meet women. Simply walking directly up to a woman and blocking her line of sight is entirely too confrontational and will usually freak girls out. You broke the Belly Button Rule because you're telegraphing too much interest. The solution? Walk up to her and either face a different direction from her or line your body up so it matches the direction she's facing and then speak to her. You can be literally standing inches away from someone when you meet them, and the direction your body faces suddenly means the difference between being a creep and a cool guy.

As you get to know a woman, obviously you'll want to face her to start building a connection. But you can play around with it by turning away from time to time to subtly play hard to get. The combination of looking at a woman eye to eye and disengaging your entire body from time to time will make you unpredictable and intriguing. Remember to keep the tension alive!

 Embody What You Say

Keep in mind you have your entire body at your disposal to communicate thoughts and ideas. As you are trying to get your points across, using physical gestures with your hands helps drive the ideas home. The key is to ensure that your gestures match up with what you're saying without coming across as nervous energy.

Here's what I mean: let's say you're giving a presentation at a business meeting about raising sales. As you mention the fact that your team increased sales from $100,000 to $125,000, you can take your hand and raise it while you mention both numbers. Another example could come from a first date with someone. As you're opening up and sharing a story from your childhood, you can take your hand and put it over your heart. For yet another example, let's say you find yourself in a conversation you're not enjoying and simply want the other person to stop talking. Raise your hand in the air like a stop sign and look away; you instantly communicate disinterest.

Instead of fidgeting with your hands and giving off nervous energy, your body can help you articulate your points. You also become a far more dynamic individual; you'll find that the most charismatic people are excellent with utilizing gestures. They truly embody what they're saying by using their entire body to share stories, make points, and capture our attention. Again, the big takeaway is to ensure that each gesture matches up with what you're saying; you don't want to be pointing and waiving your hands all over the place while you talk about a quiet, low-key moment.

Mastering this concept is really how you tie what you have just read together and demonstrate elite body language. The more engaging and dynamic you are with your expressions, the more interesting and charismatic people will find you. This is what makes actors such engaging individuals; they are experts at utilizing their entire body to communicate ideas.

Remember that our species evolved from a history of relying on our physiology to transmit information. We feel the most connected to people who fully embody what they're saying. Rather than holding back your expressions from fear of rejection, do everything at 100%. Practice becoming "overly animated" and see the type of reactions you get. What you once considered "way over the top" is actually going to connect more readily with whom you speak to. This is because we have become all too accustomed to lazy physiological expressions. It requires much more energy to fully embody what we want to say rather than simply saying it. But people aren't wired to respond to talking heads; they're wired to respond to full body performances. So use as much of your body as possible to communicate your thoughts and you'll immediately notice a sharp change in how others respond to you.

 **Easy Mistakes**

To go along with everything I just recommended, there's plenty you need to avoid. Get rid of these mistakes immediately:

- Cracking your knuckles

- Licking your lips too much

- Crossing your arms unconsciously

- Looking at your cell phone constantly

- Using too many hand gestures

- Shuffling your feet/taking small steps

- Nervous laughter

- Holding your head down submissively

Even though this chapter was short, I gave you a ton of information here. I suggest chunking it down into bite size chunks to make it more manageable. Go out and work on one thing at a time. Today work on smiling. Tomorrow work on taking up space. Then for the next day, work on eye contact. Continue coming back to this chapter and reading it often; we're trying to incorporate new habits and behaviors that your brain isn't used to doing. It takes REPETITION to ingrain these concepts into your natural behaviors.

So with that being said, let's talk about talking...

5

TALK SMOOTH, SPEAK EASY

"Good conversation is what makes us interesting. After all, we spend a great deal of our time talking and a great deal of our time listening. Why be bored, why be boring – when you don't have to be either?" – Edwin Newman

Men naturally have a more difficult time carrying on conversation than women. There are many theories as to why this persists but the one that makes the most sense to me comes from what we did as kids. While we were out competing against one another in sports and imaginary battlefields, the girls were talking with one another, having imaginary tea time and playing social games. They gained a considerable head start on their social skills and from a young age, learned how to talk with one another more easily.

Well I think it's time to play catch up. A study published by the Carnegie Institute of Technology reports that 15% of financial and career success is due to technical skills and training and 85% is due to interpersonal skills and confidence in communicating with others.[13] This tells me that you can know everything there is to know in your field, but if you are poor at getting that information across, you're putting a big lid on your potential. Whether you're a seasoned pro or a complete rookie, this chapter is going to leave you capable of carrying incredible conversations so the 85% will be no issue for you.

You're about to learn:

- How to master vocal tonality to create powerful first impressions

- Simple techniques to help you lead every conversation with ease

- How to gain command over your voice

- How to persuade and influence others

- How to speak effortlessly without running out of things to say

 ## Voice and Tone

Let's start by examining how you speak. When you talk, make sure you speak from the belly and not the nose. You can tell if someone is speaking from their nose because they sound nasally, whiny, and feminine. When you talk from your stomach, your voice has resonance and you sound more powerful and composed. Nasally peoples' voices actually vibrate at an annoying frequency that create unease (think Jerry Lewis in The Nutty Professor). In contrast, by speaking with more bass, your voice resonates in someone else's ears and the rich tones vibrate the cells in their body. Your voice is much more soothing and compelling (think George Clooney).

In terms of volume, you absolutely must be LOUD and CLEAR. Project your voice so that people can always hear you - even in crowded venues. In noisy places like bars or nightclubs, raise your voice so you don't just talk *to* people. Talk THROUGH them.

Imagine you're trying to talk to someone three feet behind whomever you're talking to. To do this, breathe from your diaphragm and push air out as you speak so your voice has more weight and carries across a further distance. Nothing can be as frustrating as having to repeat yourself when your words are trailing off, so project your voice and make it as BIG as possible when necessary.

It's funny growing up how we were so conditioned to stay quiet and "use our indoor voices." This is fine when you're in a library or need to be respectful of silence, but it doesn't carry over to public gatherings when it can be hard to hear you. While a loud, obnoxious guy can be annoying for obvious reasons, a quiet, low energy guy can be equally aggravating. It communicates a lot of things at once: you're not confident enough to be heard by others, you aren't willing to raise your energy to communicate clearly, and you will probably fold if faced with intimidation. People also don't know how to read you; are you hiding something by flying so low under the radar?

The human brain is always filtering out hundreds and thousands of unnecessary noises in an environment so it can focus on what might be potentially exciting, dangerous, provocative, unique, new, and enticing (otherwise it would pay attention to everything and drive us insane). When you don't speak loudly enough, you run the risk of being drowned out by more stimulating noises and getting rejected by the brain's filter. In contrast, when you speak with high volume, you pass this threshold more often because you generate enough energy to warrant attention. Many times, by just being the loudest person of the group, you will be seen as the leader because you command the most attention when you talk.

Whether you're in a rowdy concert with 20,000 screaming fans or in a coffee shop on a date, speak clearly and slowly without mumbling. People who talk too quickly are annoying because their frantic energy usually means they are nervous. Worse still, this habit robs you of your masculinity because it's an extremely feminine trait. So make sure you slow...down...your...delivery. Act as if you have all the time in the world to speak. Even if you are genuinely nervous, slowing down what you say will actually calm you down; remember that our emotions mirror our physiology. As an added bonus, thoughtful pauses between words create intrigue and curiosity because people will anticipate what you will say next.

If you have a deep voice (like I do) you may hear other people telling you that you mumble often (like I did). Because you and I speak with more bass in our voice, we face a greater challenge with articulating and "punching" our words. Here's what I suggest: record yourself speaking and get a sense of the difference between how you THINK you sound and how others ACTUALLY hear you. You will be amazed by the discrepancy. Then either raise the energy behind your words or look to punctuate the consonants more.

You can then take it a step further and experiment with creating a rhythm to your speech. President Obama is a master at this – watch any of his speeches and you will notice a command over rhythm and pacing. He pauses at key moments to reel you in and speaks with a certain cadence to create poetry with his words. Adding a splash of this here and there to your own style can be beneficial – just don't over do it and sound like a Baptist preacher.

Also be sure to keep your words concise and to the point. Use precision language by eliminating filler words such as "umm...like...err...ya know" from your vocabulary entirely. Complete your thoughts one sentence at a time and if you lose your train of thought, just pause for a few seconds, gather your ideas, and then continue. The more precise you are with your words, the more attention you can capture in a conversation. Think about it this way: if only 60% of your content is the intended message and 40% is filler, you guarantee that people will only listen to 60% of what you say! If you struggle with this, utilize the suggestion for those who mumble: record yourself speaking, count how often you drop an "umm" or "like" into your sentences, and then make conscious adjustments.

In addition, you should feel completely comfortable with silences and gaps in conversation. Instead of thinking, "Oh man this is awkward right now," and scrambling to fill in the gap, just smile and relax. There's no need to ever worry about quiet moments – welcome them into your conversations. In actuality, it can be rather funny to intentionally create a quiet moment in your discussion and then calmly look towards whom you're speaking to like, "What are you going to say now?"

Vocal Tonality

Vocal tonality plays an integral part in the first impression you create when you meet someone new. If you can practice and master this concept, you can actively influence what new connections think of you in a matter of seconds. Naturally, getting comfortable with applying this technique to your life will require an adjustment period. Your social instincts and habits will kick in and tempt you to return to your comfort zone, but if you stick with it, this method will become automatic for you.

There are three tonalities we speak in depending on who we're talking to, what the circumstances are, and what is at stake in the conversation. They are:

- Question Tonality

- Statement Tonality

- Command Tonality

The Question Tonality makes your voice curve up as you end the sentence. Your voice naturally does this when you ask questions. You use it when you like someone and are trying to be friendly or build rapport with them. The best example of when you use this is when you're speaking to your grandmother.

The Statement Tonality allows your voice to remain neutral throughout the sentence. Your voice naturally does this when you make statements. You use it when you're hanging out with your friends and make observations. You don't sound as nice and friendly as you do when you're using the Question Tonality, but you don't sound cold either. It's neutral.

The Command Tonality makes your voice curve down as you end your sentences. Your voice naturally does this when you command people to do things or challenge them. You use this if you're coaching a team, organizing an event, or speaking frankly. Notice in these scenarios, you're often the leader or the authority. You sound as if you're almost trying to break rapport with them – like you're not there to make friends.

The key to utilizing this information comes from knowing when each tonality is appropriate to implement in conversation. This depends on the type of first impression you would like to make with another person. Rather than floating through each interaction without a gameplan, you should actively choose which tonality you want to bring out to influence the discussion.

The Question Tonality should be reserved for talking to only those you admire, deeply love, and respect. If whom you are talking with does not meet all three of these criteria, you should not be speaking with this tone of voice - doing so makes you sound subservient and as if you are trying to please them. If you use this tone of voice when you're talking to your boss, you sound like a 'Yes Man.' If you're getting to know an attractive woman for the first time, you sound like an approval-seeking doormat. If you're trying to win over a potential client, you sound like you're trying too much to earn their business.

Here's something that's going to sound contradictory: if your goal is to impress someone else, NEVER speak as if you're trying to build rapport with them. I'll say that again in a different way: if your goal is to impress another person, *NEVER* speak with the Question Tonality. Why? Because you subconsciously give away all of your power when you're talking like this! Remember in chapter three how I discussed how important it is to master the art of Tension vs. Desire. By using the Question Tonality exclusively, you kill off all tension just about as quickly as outright saying, "I sure hope you approve of what I'm saying because I need you to like me."

For most of your interactions, you should stick with the Statement or Command Tonalities. They help position you as a social leader who assumes rapport from those he speaks with rather than someone who tries to earn it. If you maintain proper body language and speak with a strong voice, you can instantly create a memorable first impression.

The next time you come across an attractive woman for the first time, use a blend of the Command and Statement Tonalities and drop the Question Tonality altogether. Notice how she responds to your leadership and indifference of approval. This is a great way to stand out from every other guy struggling for her attention and she'll begin to wonder if YOU are APPROVING *her*. This ramps up the tension she feels with you, and as long as you aren't coming off too coldly, you will create instant attraction. Just please remember to smile and remain playful with her – it can be easy to be overly serious with these tonalities, so keep the content light.

Experiment with these two tonalities often - the next time you have a job interview, begin working with a new boss, make a business pitch to a prospective customer, meet a potential competitor, or negotiate the price of a new car, consider this your ace in the sleeve. As you become more accustomed to speaking this way, you will be surprised by how radically different others treat you. They will feel like more is at stake with you, that they should behave on their best behavior around you, and that rejecting you on any level is not a very smart idea.

As a word of caution: be sure to incorporate loose, relaxed body language when you are doing this. If you're coming across too harshly, you're just going to turn off people who won't want to be around you. I'm not suggesting you morph into a drill sergeant here. If you throw in some sincere smiles here and there, you can produce an absolutely KILLER combination. Doing this communicates confidence oozing out of your pores.

 Conversational Skills

Ralph Waldo Emerson once said, "every action is measured by the depth of the sentiment from which it proceeds." In every conversation, we experience a cycle of expression, feedback, and interpretation. Each stage of the cycle is ultimately affected by the emotions you and another person are feeling.

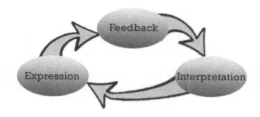

When you communicate a thought, the person you're speaking with listens to you and then responds with feedback. Your mind then processes what the feedback means and how it affects you. Whatever meaning your brain gives you ultimately affects your emotions and state of mind, influencing your next expression. This cycle repeats continuously throughout each conversation.

Even if you don't consciously sense that your emotions have been affected, everything another person says impacts you on some level - your mood either swings up or down. This then directly affects what you say next; if you're in a good mood and enjoying the conversation, words are going to flow effortlessly. If you're in a poor mood and do not like what's being said, you're going to tighten up and close off.

For example, if you're talking with a coworker – let's call him Karl - and he compliments you for wearing a new suit, you will naturally feel better; what he told you will probably be interpreted as a positive. Let's suppose you're talking to Karl later on and he tells you, "Sheesh, the economy isn't looking any better...they might start firing people here," you will probably feel much worse.

Notice that even though Karl did not overtly try to bring you down in the last example, you associated something negative with him. The content of his conversation and his likely negative mood put a damper on your emotions. If you interpret this reminder of how poorly the economy is doing as a VERY BAD thing, you're going to close up and become stifled. Your body language will project this as you will be less willing to make eye contact, you might fidget with something on your desk, and you won't smile much (if at all).

Something will feel *off* between you and the vibe you had going on will disappear.

Throughout the course of the day, we have hundreds of interactions that affect our emotions. Some conversations cheer us up and we realize we enjoy another person's company. Then some conversations irritate, sadden, anger, or bore us and we start wishing the other person wasn't around as much. We tend to let these negative interactions slide as long as he is also talking about things we enjoy. However, if someone is routinely lowering our mood over a length of time, we will begin to resent his presence.

This brings up an important point. When we go to sleep at night, seldom do we remember much of what was said to us – it's usually just bits and pieces. But we ALWAYS remember how the people we talked to made us FEEL. Therefore, your number one priority in talking with your friends, romantic partners, family members, and coworkers is to simply make sure what you say positively affects their mood. If you can train yourself to come back to this simple concept frequently during your conversations, you will consistently be a source of great emotions in others.

Social Intelligence

The key to getting the most out of this information is to master this simple concept:

- To be more likeable with others, speak only about topics that will make them feel better and avoid content that might damage their mood at almost all costs.

I say "almost all costs" because there are obviously times when you need to tell someone a truth that cannot be sugarcoated or ignored. (More on this later).

In Daniel Goleman's book *Social Intelligence*, the author explains that socially intelligent people are aware of how they affect others and intuitively understand how to create more favorable emotions in those they talk to. Socially unintelligent people, on the other hand, are often totally ignorant about the impact their words have on others and tend to continue blabbering on about topics their audience does not appreciate.[14]

You might be thinking this information is extremely basic and obvious. Yet, how many conversations can you count this past week alone that you wish you could have escaped from?

I had one roommate years ago that was so insecure he felt the need to share as many "look how cool I am" stories as he could with me to win over my approval. After the eighth or ninth tale of his unbridled "greatness," I became so bored and sick of his neediness I started stonewalling him just to see how he would respond. I figured that he would eventually get the picture and shut up altogether. I couldn't have been more wrong. Even with me barely nodding my head and saying nothing more than "cool story bro," he never shut up. I wasn't the only one who got sick of being around him; frequently at parties, he would try to meet women with this tactic and would consistently embarrass himself in front of them. He was a social disaster.

What he failed to realize was that not everyone shares the same desire to engage in what we may want to talk about, especially if it's self-centered or negative. So if you choose conversations that elevate people's moods and are highly aware when what you're talking about is falling flat, you'll have a much easier time getting into flow and building connections.

Share jokes, unique insight and knowledge, positive news, what you or the other party are passionate about and interested in, sincere praise and compliments, and entertaining stories - as long as who you speak to shows receptive body language. As soon as you notice eyes drifting, bodies fidgeting, and short responses thrown your way, change topics IMMEDIATELY.

You need to cut out all complaining, sharing of bad news (unless necessary), gossip, judgment of others, bragging, and self-defeating statements from your conversations. No one likes bearers of bad news, chronic gossipers, incessant complainers, and self-centered egotists. While complaining helps us get things off our chest and can feel good to be heard, you have to be mindful of how you affect the other person's mood.

Here is the caveat: if you absolutely have to complain or say something negative, tell the person what you're feeling beforehand

87

so he has a heads up. Give him context about what you're about to communicate. You can say, "Will you let me vent to you for two minutes? I have a lot on my mind." He will oblige you, and because you show awareness of the fact that what you're saying is unfavorable, will appreciate you caring about his mood.

Be wary of gossip and spreading negativity about other people when talking to colleagues. You run the risk of assuming the person you are talking to shares your beliefs about the other party, and if they don't, you're going to rub them the wrong way. Even worse, you'll find that the more you judge the world, the more the world will tend to judge you. So be selective about bringing up what you don't like about a person behind his back. Sitting down with him one on one is always the better course of action.

You Train People How to Talk to You

Let's jump back to the annoying roommate story. If I knew then what I know now, I would have taken some different steps in handling him. For one, I should have realized that body language alone wasn't going to get the idea through to him. After thinking back on multiple times in my life where I was dealing with someone being overly negative, weird, or boring, stonewalling them never seemed to work; in fact, it seemed to invite them to continue talking.

A more effective strategy is to simply let them get to a stopping point and then change the subject altogether. Or, if their long-winded story is just too much, another solution is to cut them off politely by summarizing what they're saying and then immediately changing the subject.

These suggestions work because we train people how to talk to us based on what we say back to them. When you change the subject to something different, they may feel initially put off, but they will quickly get the picture. The last thing you want to do is to shut down when someone is boring you with a long-winded train of thought because they will only stop talking when they decide to. Unless the person has a high enough degree of social intelligence to notice you looking disinterested, they are going to carry on because you allow them to. So simply put your foot down, change the subject, and move things along. I usually prefer to do so with a question – it engages the person's mind and requires them to respond, locking the new conversation into place.

Here's what that looks like in dialogue:

Him: "I don't think we're going to have jobs after this week. We're all screwed. I know he's going to fire me. You too probably. I mean you got here after I did – at least I have that going for me. My wife is going to kill me. I'll probably have to get a divorce because she's going to throw me out of the house for sure. I think you're gonna have to--"

You: "So you're worried about getting fired. I get it – that makes a lot of sense with what's going on. Totally understand. Hey, I need a new suit though - do you know of any good tailors around here?"

If they try to get back on subject again, go right back to square one. Interrupt them if necessary, summarize what's being said, and then ask another question. If this persists long enough, then just sit them down and tell them you're fed up with hearing what they're whining about. Simple.

This comes with a BIG disclaimer: this does not give you the right to cut people off as often as you want to when the conversation doesn't suit your needs. This is a last resort option only to be used with people who are consistently annoying, negative, and boring.

With that being said, you should also be looking to reinforce what you like talking about. If someone compliments you, don't dilute it by immediately returning the favor. Society has a habit of receiving a compliment and then immediately responding with "you too." This weakens the praise we get because we really just deflect it back to the other person. The feedback they receive can then be interpreted as you rejecting or deflecting their expression of saying something positive about you! So when someone says something nice about you, just say "thank you." People do not hear these words often enough and will respond with more sincere compliments for you in the future.

Likewise, if you enjoy talking about a particular subject, reinforce it throughout the dialogue. Let them know, "I'm really glad you brought that up" and respond with a nice big smile. With enough conditioning, you should make it abundantly obvious what you do and do not enjoy talking about. Just make sure you proactively influence the direction of each conversation.

Be a Better Listener

If there is one thing almost everyone can improve on, this is it. In fact, the vast majority of us are TERRIBLE listeners. We tend to focus almost entirely on what WE want to say instead of what the other person is expressing. This will damage your relationships on a significant level if you don't genuinely pay attention to those who matter to you.

Imagine a spotlight shining on you when you're speaking and then shining on the other person when you're listening. The last thing you want to do is hog the spotlight and keep it on your self constantly. So instead of talking *at* people as if it were a monologue, talk *with* them and keep conversation an ongoing dialogue. Take time to consider someone else's input and give them the space to direct conversational flow. Then ask questions that shift the spotlight to the other party and get them opening up.

Your goal is to show CURIOSITY about what's going on in their world. If you simply use fewer phrases that contain the words "I" and "me" and more that have "you" and "your," people will invest more of their energy into the conversation. When everything is "I did this...I think this...this happened to me...I hate this, etc." you stifle someone else's desire to add to the conversation.

The easiest way to make new friends is to use the technique of elaboration and reflection. Simply listen to what someone is telling you and then ask for more information on what they are clearly interested in. Then when they elaborate, reflect it back to them. Here's what that looks like:

THEM: I just started writing my book last week about raising children and it's going pretty well.

YOU: What inspired you to write about raising kids?

THEM: I don't know...I guess I just feel like my parents weren't always around to care for me and my brother and I saw how it affected us growing up. I want to make sure today's parents know how important it is to show that they love their kids and send the right messages...you know?

YOU: Absolutely. So you wanted to write this book to help teach parents how to balance their own obligations with giving their children support and guidance?

THEM: Exactly!

Reflecting back what someone tells you is a beautiful way of shifting the spotlight back onto them and it shows you genuinely care about what they are saying. If you're in a conversation with someone and you don't know how to respond, use the art of reflection to keep the flow going. Just paraphrase what they said in your own words and ask them to elaborate. People will love talking to you because you make them feel comfortable sharing what they are interested in.

Even if you think of yourself as the most boring, sheltered guy in the known universe, you will always come across as INTERESTING if you are truly INTERESTED in exploring someone else's passions and hobbies. In fact, the socially savvy man is not one who impresses you with his wealth of knowledge and great accomplishments. He is the man that pulls these things out of others – asking questions, reflecting their words back to them, and listening with a present mind.

Play the role of detective and dig into a person's world - notice as many details as you can. Then infuse these details into your conversations with that person as often as possible. Drop their name into conversation, comment on what they're wearing, speak to their body language, ask about events that happened without them bringing it up, and compliment them on how they have arranged their appearance. If you fully engage as a great listener and are aware of these details most people miss, you will make it virtually impossible for anyone to forget you.

Vibing

In most social situations, the entire point of conversation is to get to know someone better and/or improve your relationship together. Think about it – when you're talking to someone, you're "vibing" with them – you're sharing thoughts and ideas in a friendly and casual way. What you're not doing is keeping a running list of errors one another is making in an attempt to see who's the "most correct."

Perhaps the biggest conversational sin you can make is getting too analytical and taking everything said literally. Correcting another person's errors does nothing to improve your friendship; in fact, it corrodes it. As soon as you allow a conversation to slide into a debate over who is "right" about a particular fact or belief, you've lost sight of the bigger picture. At that point, it's not really even about who's "right" - it's about whose ego needs the most nurturing.

For example, if someone is talking about rock climbing and you feel that you are an expert at it, when they share information you believe is wrong, you are going to feel the urge to correct them. You are going to want to prove to them how much more you know about it and how better you are at it. You will notice your ego wanting to butt in and dominate the lesser intelligence. But let it slide; as good as it feels to put someone in their place, it pales in comparison to how you much you have ruined the social vibe.

Remember that no one remembers much of the content from their daily interactions. I guarantee you no one goes to bed at night thinking, "I'm so grateful he showed me how to do a proper figure eight follow through knot and prove how wrong I was. What a nice guy." If anything, they are going to sleep irritated that you tried to show them up without any courtesy or respect. Life is not a pissing contest – it's not about "winning" arguments. No matter how ingenious your analysis might be, no one ever wants to engage in these meaningless battles.

There are two styles of discussion that *every single one* of our conversations fall into:

- Serious/Literal

- Playful/Sarcastic

Serious discussions take place when two people are sharing information they want each other to interpret matter-of-factly. Such as: financial figures, scientific data, problem-solving, and important conversations they want honest feedback about.

Playful discussions take place when two people are often joking or simply talking in a relaxed fashion with no clear goal in mind. Such as: sarcastic jokes, witty banter, and small talk. These conversations take place when our goal is to vibe with one another and keep the material light and relaxed.

I have noticed a fair share of my friends throughout my life were only capable of using one style exclusively. My highly intelligent buddies could not seem to ever slip out of the serious style and couldn't, for the life of them, understand sarcasm. If we took a tour of Japan and I noticed how crowded it was, if I said something like, "Wow – there's like a trillion people here..." I would get answers like, "Well, actually, there's only 127 million." *Gee, thanks buddy.*

Likewise, I've had friends whom I could never seem to take seriously even with important life-changing decisions on the line. These are the guys who I've sat down with asking for advice on taking a life-altering job or graduating from college with a degree, and having them simply shrug their shoulders, laugh, and change the subject to a sarcastic joke about the new Will Ferrell movie.

If you want to feel confident in both business and social venues, you must be comfortable switching between styles and understanding when each one is appropriate. If you are extremely intelligent and notice that you just don't enjoy joking or talking in a playful tone, you need to learn how to loosen up. Recognize that when people are vibing, they're just looking to feel good with no greater goal in mind. These situations do not warrant cold analysis or fact correction.

If, on the other hand, you are able to keep small talk going and love making sarcastic comments non-stop, balance your humor with the courage to speak seriously when needed. You never want to see a close friend come to you with an important decision and find yourself unable to offer any true support. As a car shifts gears smoothly and effortlessly when needed, you should be prepared for new directions your conversations shift into as well.

When people recognize you have these two distinct sides to you, your value increases. You are versatile enough to clown, goof off, and joke, but also capable of tackling serious and important discussions. This makes you infinitely more valuable as a friend simply because you can be trusted with the full spectrum of conversation. Your buddies will be more inclined to invite you out for drinks and also ask you to join them for business networking events.

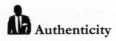 **Authenticity**

Speaking with authenticity is one of the most difficult things we face, but it is a necessary part of maintaining integrity. To do so, you must speak what feels most true to you in each moment without changing what you are going to say based on how someone else might react. I understand this is easier said than done; the challenge in following through on this idea comes with the fear that many people will not appreciate your honesty. Yet in order to really embody your beliefs and stand for what is important to you, you have to develop the courage to speak your truth when necessary.

I believe humanity's greatest fear (aside from public speaking and death) is the fear of offending others. This probably stems from the scolding we received from our parents when we were kids every time we spoke up and "offended someone else." While we were taught how to be polite and kind, our young minds were forming several connections between what we were saying and how society might interpret our thoughts. One of the beliefs that we unfortunately latched onto was probably something along the lines of: "When I speak out and say what I'm really thinking, I hurt someone else, so I shouldn't do it anymore." While this is not altogether a terrible thing because kids have a habit of yelling out rude and obnoxious observations in public without proper supervision, this conditioning stunts our willingness to speak our minds and carries over into adulthood. We have such a strong need for others to not take offense to our thoughts that we tend to perform our best chameleon impersonation to avoid conflict.

But here's a wake up call: not everyone likes you, will like you, or has liked you. In fact, a variety of people throughout your life have disliked you and you haven't even known it.

I know this sounds harsh. Here's the good news: you are going to offend people throughout your life no matter what you do - not because your intention is to disturb them or cause them harm, but because everyone on the planet approaches life with a unique viewpoint. What you say isn't going to jibe with every single person you come into contact with and there is really nothing you can do about it. So rather than trying to win over the approval of everyone, win over the approval of those who appreciate your authenticity the most. Say what you feel must be said when you feel you need to say it instead of what others would like to hear in a given moment.

I want to make this very clear: I'm not suggesting you now have the right to go about life freely sharing each of your opinions as you see fit. This is not about you going on a quest to prove how "right" you are about everything and shooting down those who disagree with you along the way. Speaking with authenticity does not mean trying to dominate each conversation until you walk away the winner. It actually means being more vulnerable - opening up and exposing what you truly believe without the expectation of changing someone else's mind. Sharing your truth is all you must do; whether another person agrees with it or not is entirely up to them.

There are moments when someone you know will need a wakeup call. You're not serving that person by tiptoeing around an issue; your honesty is needed more than your politeness. If your best friend has openly told you that he's cheating on his wife and you feel like he's running a serious risk of ruining what you believe to be a wonderful marriage, you must speak authentically and bring

95

this up to him. You can't continue hanging out with him as this hovers over both of your heads without being discussed. Forget about whether or not he disagrees and might become antagonistic with you. Situations like these call for brutal honesty and ignoring them ultimately destroys your relationships.

You will also come across situations where you must stand up for someone not present in the room. If a conversation within your social group turns to gossiping about a mutual friend or colleague, you need to protect that person's reputation if you believe what's being said is false. This can mean being the only person in the group who doesn't take part in the "fun" and playing the role of buzzkill. If this feels like too much difficulty, think about how much you would appreciate someone else backing you up if others were talking about you behind your back. You will never regret behaving like a bigger man in these moments.

So call it like you see it - if there is something that you feel needs to be addressed, bring it up regardless of how others might react. Keep the connection between your heart and your mouth open and never be afraid to speak what is real to you. Your truth is something you intuitively feel and comes from a place of love and service, not from a need of approval or even acknowledgment. One of the greatest gifts you can give the world is an honesty that expects nothing in return. Give it freely with confidence.

Don't Sell Out

Assuming you're not doing something heinous like cheating on your wife, no one has the right to make you feel guilty about your decisions or beliefs. When you alter who you are to suit someone else's needs and win over their approval, you are SELLING OUT. You are BUYING their acceptance with the illusion that caving into their guilt will make you happier.

Whether you still feel like you need to live up to your parent's expectations, want to impress a friend, or get along with a new woman you're seeing, any time you behave differently than you truly want to, you're being inauthentic. People smell inauthenticity from miles away, and instead of it making you more likeable, it makes them want to ignore and disrespect you. Why? Because you're forgoing your own unique personality to be someone you're not.

It's funny how often we make up white lies if our friends invite us to do things we really don't feel like doing. How many times have you made something up just because you felt guilty about shooting down the offer? Here's a new idea: instead of throwing out the old "I'll see if I can come – I know I'm going to be very busy" excuse, just tell the person NO. Shocking isn't it? You'd be amazed how much this little tweak simplifies your life. Contrary to what you might think, your friends will actually appreciate your honesty and will feel connected to your authenticity.

If you love taking part in or talking about a particular hobby and then run into someone who talks poorly of it or even asks you to stop doing it, never cave into their demands - especially if they use guilt as their primary tactic. Tell them they're just going to have to deal with it and then do it even more! Just because someone does not share your preferences or passions doesn't mean they ever have the right to control your behavior. Trust me, you're doing yourself a huge favor by ignoring these attempts at manipulation.

People use guilt in a variety of ways to control you. They say, "Be realistic" to guilt you into following the herd and not blazing your own trail. They say, "Everyone else is doing it" to guilt you into behaving a certain way to match society's standards. They say, "You must not love me enough" to guilt you into doing a favor that is entirely inconvenient to you. These ploys work because most of us have been so conditioned to avoid offending others that we can mistakenly believe we are being rude and abrasive by not caving in. However, guilt alone is never a good enough reason to do something – either you decide to do it or not.

Once you have made up your mind, you need to shut down any attempts at guilting you into going against your decision immediately. As soon as someone begins whining, cut them off and say, "Wait a second – this sounds like you're trying to guilt me into doing this against my own will. Are you trying to make me feel guilty now?" This should throw a wrench in their plans, but if they still persist, follow up with, "OK – it *really* sounds like you're trying to make me feel guilty. Since you are obviously trying to control me, I am *definitely* not going to do it now." This is the equivalent of stiff-arming the guilt trip and dumping it back on the other person's head.

Phillip Johnson once said, "People don't like it when you change because the ways they used to manipulate you stop working." You'll find that any time you veer off course against the wishes of your friends and family, they will resent you for it. The vast majority of the world does not have the courage to follow their intuition in spite of their close ones disagreeing with them. Usually a little guilt is all that is necessary to convince someone to settle and return to the same path their loved ones are comfortable with. From this moment forward, you must be a stand for doing what is right according to your beliefs and values and not allow the fears and doubts of others to become your measuring stick.

Being truly authentic means relying on your own guidance in spite of what others may think of your choices. You have to be willing to go against the grain of the tribe. Listen, I'm not advocating to live your life carelessly or to ignore your support group just for the sake of being contrary. What I am suggesting, however, is that there will be opportunities in your life to make changes in uncharted territory. Rather than caving into the illusion of "being realistic" according to someone else's standards, be practical according to what makes the most sense for you. You develop this power of intuition by making your decisions match your inner desires – no matter what others tell you.

How to Never Run Out of Things to Say

Keep in mind that out of any given sentence you speak, your audience forgets roughly 80-90% of the words immediately. Instead of memorizing every word that rolls off your tongue, the people you talk to are simply gathering the *gist* of your point.

Remember this if you find yourself in situations where you don't quite know what to say next in conversation. Speaking with authenticity involves not having to think so much about what's going to flow out of your mouth and just trusting that whatever does will be appropriate to the situation as intended. When you relax and just let thoughts flow from within, you communicate in a far simpler and natural way.

You don't have to have entire sentences formulated in your head before you open your mouth. It's OK to even have absolutely no idea what you're going to end up talking about. Just trust that you're going to find it naturally and let the gist come to you. When I'm coaching with my clients over the phone, I tend to routinely start sharing advice with only about 25% of an idea fleshed out in my mind. I find that the other 75% just flows naturally from my intuition in a way that bypasses my brain entirely. The more you practice speaking this way, the more you will realize that your mind can actually slow down your communication more than enhance it. Rather than forcing every idea to check in with it, let your thoughts naturally show up and express them as they come.

I'm going to ask you to play a game if you're the type of person who struggles even occasionally with knowing what to say next in conversation. It's called the Two Second Rule. The rules are simple: the next time you are talking to someone new, force yourself to say the first thing that comes to mind within two seconds of dead time. No matter how stupid it is, no matter how off subject it is, and no matter how random it is. The point of this game is to realize how easy it is to connect with someone and trust that they will be able to handle the gist of what you throw at them while keeping conversation flowing.

Some of the most confident networkers and businessmen I've met are masters at this. While most people hesitate to change the topic and cling to boring statements about the weather and what each other does for a living, these conversationalists vary the subject constantly. What I've found is that even if someone can't keep up with them, they are far more engaged in the discussion. By jumping around different subjects when they first meet someone, they are able to quickly decipher what one another has in common, how and if they can be of help to each other, and who they can introduce to one another.

Just simply lower the bar for how constructed you feel each sentence must be and expect people to easily respond to whatever you throw at them. Realize that even in the most stimulating conversations over half of what both of you say will probably be "filler" anyways. Who cares! Think of the filler as the bridges you need to build in order to get to new topics.

One last point: throughout each conversation, defend your initiative to speak. When you begin a sentence, even if someone else chimes in or tries to interrupt you, finish your sentence. Stay on your train of thought. This is one of the easiest ways to determine how highly someone values their own opinions. If they stop talking the moment someone else butts in, it's obvious they don't believe what they're saying is important. So practice focusing on your train of thought while you speak and finish it *even as* another person chimes in. This keeps the flow of your thoughts running smoothly and allows you to keep talking without losing momentum.

 Verbal Influence

So far we've covered how you can confidently communicate with others and maintain smooth conversations. This section aims to give you some extra ammunition for the times when you need to defend yourself, change someone's mind, or negotiate to find a middle ground. Understanding the key components of verbal influence means having a secret weapon available when needed. Whether you're talking to a bouncer to let you and your friends into a club, negotiating for a higher salary, or trying to talk someone out of making a mistake, you have an edge unavailable to most. As an added benefit, you will become more aware of when others are trying to manipulate or persuade you and will be able to use this knowledge to defend yourself when necessary.

With that being said, it is not my goal in sharing this information for you to use it to take advantage of others. These are powerful techniques you can utilize to influence another person's decisions in a highly efficient and direct way. I'm trusting you will be able to draw the line and not cross it.

Command Language

Your ability to not only maintain smooth conversations but to also LEAD them directly impacts how successful you are. If you don't have this skill in place, you're severely limiting your influence and what's possible for you in every major aspect of your life. You want to become a master at influencing the direction of your conversations.

Command language is powerful because it is human nature to crave certainty and a sense of confident direction with whom we speak with. People rely on strong decision-making in social situations and almost always default to the social leader when choices are up in the air. By utilizing this technique, we can immediately position ourselves as the authority in a conversation and persuade others to listen to us. We do this by embedding commands into what we're saying without coming off as bossy or pushy.

You can easily take advantage of this concept by implementing three of my favorite words: "let's do this."

For example, if you're on a date with a woman who hasn't been agreeing with you about your dinner options, you can resolve the issue by saying, "Let's do this: let's go to this restaurant that I love and I know you will love first, then you can pick dessert somewhere else." Notice the wording – you're NOT asking for her permission to go to this restaurant. You're not saying, "Can we go here? Is it OK if we go here?" Any time the person you're speaking with is unsure of a course of action, by simply saying, "let's do this..." you give them a specific direction to take with you. Because you're confident when you say this, more often than not, they will follow your lead.

Most people are looking for someone to take them by the hand and lead them. Remember that many people avoid offending others at all costs and actively seek permission to do what they want to do. Knowing this, you can actually flat out tell people what's going to happen on your terms, and based on how strongly you believe it, they will go along with it.

Let's say you're looking for a new apartment to move into and your potential landlord tells you it's going to cost two-thousand dollars. Say, "I'll do sixteen-hundred." When he tells you something like, "No, I can't go that low – I have it priced at two-thousand," you can flatly say, "I understand." Then you can look him in the eyes and say, "I'll give you eighteen-hundred for it, and two full months rent in advance for it now." What's the worst that can happen? More than likely, he's going to cave into your determination and give you a discount on the price. If not, who cares?

Practice gently commanding people as often as you can. If a friend wants to go to a restaurant you're not too fond of, just say, "Let's go here instead." If a salesman is pressuring you into a decision you're not sure of, just say, "Here's what's going to happen. I'm going to buy this at five hundred or you're about to lose a sale." If you simply tell people what to do, they're usually going to cooperate as long as you're being reasonable.

Another way to use command language is to suggest that someone agrees with you. This is particularly powerful if used sparingly. For example, let's say you'd like to see a co-worker show up with you to karaoke night with the rest of the office but he's extremely shy and introverted. Instead of just diving into the request, get him to agree with you first. Do this by saying, "You're an open-minded guy, right? And you're open to exploring new things as long as the people involved fully support you, right?" He will respond with a yes to both questions (who wouldn't?), which allows you to then command him to come with you in a way that makes sense: "Great – then you're definitely coming to karaoke night. Grab your stuff."

The more you ASSUME and EXPECT people to follow your suggestions, the more they will march to the beat of your drum. Remember that people are used to others making decisions for them; the more certain you are about a specific course of action, the more likely you will influence their choices. So simply assume a person will go along with you – because they usually will (as long as you're not being ridiculous).

AIRE

AIRE is an acronym you can think of as a gameplan for handling a disagreement someone is having with you. Each letter stands for a specific step you will take to handle the issue and then move on. The formula is:

Acknowledge

Investigate

Reiterate

Educate

If you simply throw back your opinion after someone expresses disagreement with you, they will automatically ignore you and try to reiterate their argument. The reason is due to the fact that you neglected to show you were actually listening to them. By first acknowledging what a person is saying, you cause them to lower their guard and be more receptive to what you have to say. You're communicating that you are truly hearing them.

To take it a step further, you can even personalize the validation by offering a sentence or two about why you personally understand where they are coming from.

For example, if your father severely disagrees with your decision to quit your job to start your own business, you can acknowledge his argument by saying something like, "Believe me, Dad. I get where you're coming from. What you're saying makes a lot of sense, and I want you to know this isn't something I just rushed into. In fact, while I was thinking about the pro's and con's of doing this, I put a lot of what you taught me into close consideration." Notice that you're taking the validation beyond a meager little sentence. You're not saying, "Yeah yeah yeah I get it, whatever." You're taking your time to show him that you value his perspective.

After you acknowledge what he is saying, your next step is to investigate where he is coming from. Here is where you play detective and get closer to the true nature of the disagreement. Your goal is to get right to the core of why they are disagreeing with you. You want to strip away any assumptions you might have been making by getting clear answers on his MAIN objection to what it is you want.

Back to the father example: "Dad, let me ask you this: is your main concern about me doing this strictly because of financial reasons?" (His response would go something like, "Well yeah, I'd hate to see you go broke or end up unable to provide for your family.") "Got it. I totally understand. And that's pretty much the biggest reason you disagree with my decision to do this?" By asking these questions, you do two things: for one, you show him that you're truly invested in understanding where he's coming from and not just brushing him off and two, you find out the one true reason he disagrees with your point of view. This makes your ability to explain your side of the story much more precise and clear.

The next step is reiteration. Here is where you show him that you are not only listening, but also fully understand where he's coming from. This allows you to reframe the disagreement into something more manageable. You accomplish this by first acting as a mirror to what he's saying: "So what you're saying is that if I decide to walk away from my job, my financial situation could change and affect how capable I am in providing for my family – and that is risky and potentially dangerous? Is that a fair assessment?"

Next, you can reframe the disagreement since you've proven that you have completely listened and understood what he has said. You do this with the final step, education. This is where you educate the person on your point of view in a way that acknowledges his one big objection and provides a solution for it.

Here is how you could wrap up the argument with your father: "I've actually been growing a list of customers who have pre-ordered my product months in advance. In fact, right now, I have over two thousand people who have already paid for what I'm making. Once I put the finishing touches on my website and incorporate into an LLC, I'll start shipping to their doors. I've made sure to plan for my monthly expenses, and I've been able to keep everything extremely low. Three months in, my profits will exceed ten thousand dollars. Now I understand that I'm just talking about the first few months, but I already have several concepts in place for future products. I feel great about the business, my wife fully supports me, and at the end of the day, this is my life. I'm prepared to live with the consequences."

Who could possibly shoot that down? You have sufficiently reflected back his side of the story, shown that you have carefully listened, discovered the number one reason for his disagreement, and then addressed that disagreement in a way that put your viewpoint into a greater perspective. This way, your father has no room to butt back in because you have totally covered his disagreement in its entirety while providing a solution that eradicates it entirely.

Just remember that people will rarely ever listen to your side of an argument until you prove to them that you have listened and understood their position. If they keep trying to interrupt your take on the story, take it as a sign that you need to slow down and show them you get what they're saying.

Ascribing Virtues

As a general rule of thumb, people will behave according to how you expect them to behave if you give them a specific role to live into. If you tell someone, "Well since I know you're not going to finish the assignment, I'm really wasting my time asking you this, but could you please finish the report by Monday?" - you set the stage for them to fail you. You're confirming their role in your partnership as being the weak, flaky one.

Instead, ascribe the virtues you want a person to live into. If you want your business partner to finish everything in a timely manner, express your confidence in him: "Since I know I can always count on you to finish what you start, I know you'll have no problem getting the report to me by Monday, right?" If you trust a person, they will tend to be honest with you and live up to your expectations. If you doubt them, they will tend to lie to you and fall short.

This is known as the Pygmalion effect – the greater the expectation placed upon people, the better they tend to perform. Putting a label on someone is a powerful tool – use it in a negative way and you set a clear intention for them to fail. You create a self-fulfilling prophecy in their mind when they take action; if you think they won't succeed, why should they? Instead, use empowering labels that give another person confidence in behaving the way you expect them to.

Be clear that ascribing a virtue to someone is one step beyond simply giving them a compliment. A compliment is short-lived praise that isn't necessarily tied to anything the person will do in the future. Think of them as brief appreciation for what a person has accomplished in the past or is currently accomplishing now. When you ascribe a virtue, you give them some specific shoes to fill and a certain role to play – it's more like a compliment in advance. It's human nature to want to behave in congruence with this type of respect; we don't want to let anyone down by not earning the approval.

Utilizing this method of verbal influence comes especially in handy when you want someone to step out of their comfort zone and attempt something new. I recently asked one of my best friends to be my best man for my wedding and I knew he would be uncomfortable giving the speech. Instead of just asking him to give the speech and hoping he would nail it, I gave him confidence in coming through in a major way. I explained that he had a specific role to play in the wedding as the best man and that this role couldn't have been filled by anyone else. Because he was one of my best friends, I told him he knew more about my relationship with my fiancé, Bethany, than anyone else at the wedding, and that he would provide the perfect speech for us. I also gave him a shot in the arm by describing the amount of confidence I had in him; I said, "Because you have a great balance of brains and heart most don't have, I know I can depend on you to deliver when it counts the most."

Sure enough, he rocked the speech and showcased the most confidence I've ever seen him possess in my life. Because I expected nothing but greatness from him, I received something great in return. Up to the wedding date, every time he brought up the subject, I reflected back positive feedback with my body language and words I chose. Whenever he looked to me for confirmation, I indicated in every way possible that he was going to be excellent. This confidence carried him through the planning and preparation and he lived up to my expectations on our special day.

Remember that people instinctively look for social proof when navigating uncharted waters. They want to see what others are doing around them to help dictate their actions. Keep this in mind the next time you ask someone to do something new: YOUR beliefs and expectations regarding their success will play a HUGE role in how they show up. When they look you in the eyes and you're thinking, "I hope he can do this – but who am I kidding?" - they will SEE and FEEL your lack of faith. You must serve as a buoy they can grab onto immediately to begin gaining certainty. Otherwise your poor expectations will not only fail to bolster confidence, but will likely demotivate them from taking action.

6

YOUR SOCIAL GAMEPLAN

"People will forget what you said, people will forget what you did, but people will never forget how you made them feel." – Maya Angelou

So now that you're aware of how to physically carry yourself and how to communicate with others confidently, let's put it all together with your social game plan. With the right tools and preparation, you can gain several lasting friendships, date beautiful women (or attract the woman of your dreams), succeed with your co-workers, throw unforgettable parties, and network like a rock star. You can apply as much or as little of this information as suitable for your tastes; if you'd rather live a more modest lifestyle with a few tight friendships here or there, this chapter will help polish your skills nonetheless.

My ultimate goal is to now prepare you to succeed in a number of environments, both friendly and hostile. You won't always find yourself in affable situations - how you handle rejection and attempts at intimidation will say a lot about your character. To become a well-rounded man, you're going to need to learn to navigate difficult or awkward social situations without allowing them to affect you. This is a skill most guys fall entirely too short with.

In this chapter, you'll learn:

- How to cultivate a rejection-proof mindset

- Why humans have the need for social acceptance and how you can take back control of your primal instincts

- A game plan for meeting more people and dating more women

- How to handle every person that tries to intimidate you

- Exactly what to say to gain immediate friendships and lasting relationships

 Social Acceptance

Thousands of years ago, before major civilizations were established, humans lived in small tight knit communities. These tribes kept us alive and protected; with no connection to a group, we would be left alone in the wilderness to fend for ourselves (which meant an almost certain death). To avoid the possibility of being outcast, our brains became hard-wired to behave with caution around those with the power to eliminate our status in the tribe. If we pissed off the alpha male of the community, we might either be killed or sent packing.

Because being an outcast was a direct threat to our survival and replication, a very clear message was programmed into our brains: AVOID ALL CHANCES OF REJECTION – REJECTION = DEATH. This is why our anterior cingulate cortex, the part of the brain activated when we endure physical pain, also gets activated in the same way when we encounter social rejection. This portion of your brain literally cannot tell the difference between a broken heart and a broken leg.

In today's world, the threat of rejection is obviously no longer a threat to our physical wellbeing. We're free to travel as we please, live wherever we desire, make new connections around the globe, and thrive in a multitude of communities. In fact, we could be socially rejected by hundreds of people on a continuous, never-ending basis, and the only threat to our survival would be mild embarrassment. Yet deep in our makeup, this outdated fear of rejection is still part of our programming, driving our behavior and dulling our confidence. We know that a lack of social acceptance is of no threat to us *logically*, but this is entirely different than living it *subconsciously*.

I'd like to challenge you to build your social circle as you please in spite of your obsolete primal instincts. In today's Facebook age, we all seem to have hundreds of "virtual friends" with fewer and fewer meaningful relationships. Communicating through a computer screen is obviously easier than displaying your true colors in public; after all, it takes courage and effort to put yourself out there. But if you understand how to meet people, create new friendships, brush off weak attempts at intimidation, and put strong conversational habits into place, you can be dropped off in a brand new town without knowing anyone and quickly create powerful connections.

These tools will aid you in developing a razor-sharp edge in a variety of social situations, including your coworkers, romantic partners, or new friendships. They will help you internalize social confidence on a subconscious level so that your behavior matches your knowledge.

Choose Whose Opinions Matter to you Wisely

Before we work on expanding your social circle, I want to discuss an important point. One of the biggest decisions you must always consider is whom you want to spend your time with. What kinds of people do you want in your social circle, what values do you want them to have, and what makes them unique?

Jim Rohn said it best, "You are the average of the five people you spend the most time with." You typically have roughly the same income, you weigh close to the same weight, you tend to dress similarly, you believe most of the same things, and you possess the same level of intelligence. The culture you surround yourself in not only rubs off on you, it *is* you.

This is because human beings constantly affect one another by playing a major part in shaping each other's lives. If your five closest friends are skilled at dating and attracting women, even if you were clueless before you met them, you're going to know a lot more about the subject by just being around them. They are going to expect you to take more action with approaching women in public places or following through on dates. They will be monitoring you more closely and giving you feedback for how you're doing more than a group of single slobs. You will constantly absorb behaviors and new beliefs from those you're closely linked to through this process of social osmosis.

I don't know about you, but I don't want to be the average of five mediocre people with no goals or ambitions. Even if you are extremely motivated and have a 'succeed at all costs' mentality, your environment can and will affect you. So if you don't truly respect or appreciate your current group of friends and the lives they are living, it's time to move on to greener pastures. This is especially important if you hang out with anyone who doesn't support your highest goals and dreams. Drop them from your circle immediately – they're toxic to your growth.

I can already hear some of you whining, "But that's just coldhearted – they're my friends!" Here's the deal: if you can't behave authentically around someone close to you without them making you feel guilty or wrong, there is no place for them in your life. Period. In fact, they aren't a friend at all – they are one of your biggest obstacles to creating the life you envision.

If you don't respect what someone values or believes (or who they are as a person), you shouldn't listen to their advice and especially to their criticism. I would advise you to completely ignore these people, especially if they try to weaken your mood. Be extremely picky about whose opinion you value and whose you don't. If you let every Joe Schmo offer you their two cents, you're going to end up taking some of it.

Conversely, if you do respect someone else and value where they are in life, either in terms of success, happiness, wealth, relationships, or health, be open to advice and suggestions from them. If someone possesses qualities that you admire and/or respect, be open to them giving you new ideas and insights into life. Here is where you want to be a sponge and absorb as much wisdom from that person as possible. Because they have the type of lifestyle that you want or are simply the kind of person you respect, their thinking will be reflective of this. So listen to it!

There's a Dr. Seuss quote I love that nails this whole idea down: "Be who you are and say what you feel because those who mind don't matter and those who matter don't mind."

Be careful about who you follow, who you feel is important to you, and who you let affect your thinking. Never let your need for being accepted in a peer group overshadow the quality of the person judging you.

The 4 Personalities

As I mentioned in the previous chapter, people can possess entirely different views of the world. Each of us has a unique set of beliefs, thoughts, emotions, and convictions. Yet, how easy is it for the world to argue with one another about the very things we know we feel differently about? It's funny that we know people value things differently from us, and yet find ourselves immediately disliking someone because they don't share the same preferences. If you can live with the fact that people will simply not like the same things you feel are important, you won't be compelled to let your ego get out of control. You'll maintain composure more often.

There have been several ways our culture has attempted to "categorize" people and I'm sure we're going to be coming up with hundreds more in the future. Although it can be stereotypical to label someone a certain personality-type and then pigeonhole them, it can also be equally useful to quickly understand where someone is coming from and then meet them on their level.

This method of categorization is known commonly as the Four Temperaments (or Four Humours). I'm going to call it the Four Personalities. They are:

- **The Go-Getters** – The type of people who drive fast cars, spend a lot of money, compete at the highest level, feel they have to win at all costs, and will do anything to be a champion. These are often the "type-A" individuals who are driven to succeed and dominate the competition. The Go-Getters love responding to challenge and proving how competitive they are.

- **The Socialites** – Party loving, fun people who want to take it easy, have a good time, and meet as many people as possible. Typically they are very outspoken and extroverted, often referred to as "social butterflies." They tend to value FUN and FEELING GOOD more than anything else.

- **The Thinkers** – Very analytical, number crunching, fact-finding people. This type of individuals doesn't like to make impulsive decisions and love analyzing things from every angle possible. They're generally more monotone in both voice and behavior; they won't wear anything to stand out and tend to avoid the Socialites.

- **The Spiritualists** – Spiritual, loving people who want everyone to get along, and who value the team concept over winning at all costs. These people can feel like possessing a lot of material goods can lead to vanity and tend to value intangible concepts and values much more. This group usually wants the world to just "get along" and often avoid competition.

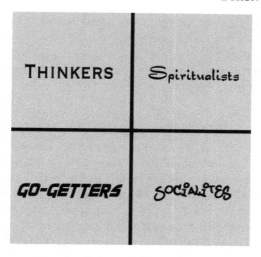

Most people tend to be a mixture of two personalities. You might be a Go-Getter Socialite who hates losing, loves dressing in high status clothing, and enjoys going out to clubs and parties to meet people. Or you might be a Spiritualist Thinker, who loves studying philosophy, thinking about life's deepest issues, and solving complex problems. Or, hey, you might fall into one main personality entirely. Take some time to consider which of these personalities you tend to take on most and then start looking for them when you meet others.

Think back to an occasion where you met someone new who seemed to just rub you the wrong way. Imagine how he talked, the way he described things, whether or not he used profanity, what he seemed to be interested in, what he looked like, and what he wanted to talk about. At the time, you probably summarized these features into one negative belief about him: "This guy's annoying/arrogant/weird/stupid/materialistic/boring, etc."

But here's what you didn't know: his core personality was probably just *different* than yours. Now he may very well have been an "arrogant, boring, weird slob," but consider the characteristics he was working with. Now that you have this information, realize that the reason you may dislike someone is simply because they have a different personality type. Think about this before you give up on developing rapport.

Of course, there will be times when people seem to reject you because they don't mesh well with your personality. Being aware that each of us possesses different core personalities, you should never feel that the person is making a sweeping statement about you as a person.

You can use this information to help you in a variety of circumstances. If you're in sales, recognize a potential client's personality type and make adjustments with how you communicate with her to get in sync. If she's a Go-Getter, you'll want to get to the point as quickly as possible in your presentation and avoid long-winded statements. Show her how the product will allow her to be the best in her field. If you're meeting your girlfriend's parents for the first time, and you notice her father is a Thinker, you'll want to go a bit lighter on the sarcasm, explain yourself in terms of logic and reason, and behave with more restraint.

This is not to say that you should change who you are to win someone else's approval. You're still expressing your authentic self without compromise. Instead, think of this as you making small tweaks to your personality that are minor adjustments to win a person over. These details make an enormous difference in building rapport and making a connection with someone.

I recommend doing a few activities that a person with the opposing personality from you would partake in to become more well-rounded. For example, if you're a Thinker, consider taking an acting class, attending a comedy workshop, or joining Toast Masters. If you're a Spiritualist, play a competitive sport, attend a rigorous physical boot camp, or start a tough workout regimen. If you identify as a Go-Getter, join a book club, donate to a charity, or attend some yoga workouts. If you consider yourself a Socialite, learn a new hobby you can practice alone, pick up a few books, or visit an academic conference.

By doing this, you stretch your self-concept in several healthy ways. For one, you're getting out of your comfort zone and growing as a man. As another added benefit, you're boosting your confidence because you're expanding the variety of environments you're comfortable in. You're also a far more interesting person; imagine telling someone you're an experienced meditator with a degree in thermodynamics who enjoys playing rugby.

Your Game Plan for Meeting People (Part 1)

As I said before, expanding your social circle is important and you need to be proactive about it. Even if you're currently satisfied with your group of buddies, keep in mind that there are always people who know more than you do in certain areas of life. Also consider that your goal should be to consistently find higher-quality people for your social circle. Rather than sitting around and waiting for these relationships to develop, take the initiative yourself.

So here are five ways you can make some new connections and increase your contact list. Implement any number of these strategies you feel are a good fit for your lifestyle.

1) Friends of Friends

Take stock of your current friends (the ones you enjoy being around) and ask them if they know anyone with similar hobbies. Coordinate parties and get-togethers on the weekend with your buddies and ask them to invite their friends along. Have your friends introduce you to their acquaintances, and then simply get to know them through the shared interest.

Often by simply increasing the quantity of new people you meet in a given week, you will increase your group of friends. The easiest way to do this is to leverage your current social circle. For every one friend you have, he or she should have at least five or six solid connections you should plan on meeting. Once you meet these people through your current mutual friends, consider then expanding to *their* five or six connections. Continue building your social life in this way and you have the potential of gaining a plethora of new peers.

For a more direct approach, think of subjects you would like to learn more about and ask your buddies, "Hey, who do you know that knows a lot about (XYZ)?" Ask for his or her number, call

117

them up, and schedule a coffee to chat. Because few people ever go out of their way to meet others like this, asking someone to help teach you about something they're interested in is a practically guaranteed way to make friends. As an added bonus, you can find out about clubs or teams a person is a part of and see about joining them.

If the person doesn't get back to you, don't take it personally; meeting people is always a risk in some shape or form – some don't have the confidence to meet people this way or feel altogether too busy. Neither are marks against you.

2) Networking

Every day in every city across the country, groups are hosting networking events to exchange business cards and meet new faces. Going to these networking events is an easy way to make professional acquaintances, create new friendships, or gain new clients.

Check out http://www.meetup.com for a list of available "Meet Up" groups in your area and make it a point to attend a local meeting when you can. This website is an excellent resource for those looking to make new connections while discussing a common business interest or hobby. Simply pick a group you feel comfortable with, pay attention to the times they meet, and attend the get-togethers when possible.

Alternatively, feel free to check out your local Chamber of Commerce (http://www.chamber.com). This is a group that hosts various meetings in cities across the country with the goal of strengthening a local business network. This is a great group to join if you own your own business and are looking for more local support.

If you live in a big city, you can simply search for networking opportunities close to you. Open up Google and search "(my city) networking" and you'll find dozens of websites to help point you in the right direction. The internet is a powerful tool for bringing people together.

3) Parties and Get-Togethers

Whether you attend barbecues, cocktail parties, group dinners, or get a group together to watch sports, accepting these invitations means meeting more people.

When you're at the party, be proactive and ask the host to introduce you to people you don't know. If the guy (or girl) hosting the gathering has any social class whatsoever, they should do a decent job introducing you and setting the stage for a potential friendship. Events like these are always easy ways to make friends and should be embraced as often as possible.

You should also consider hosting these get-togethers from time to time. Playing host allows you to connect different sets of your own friends and see them expanding their social circles. If you throw a great party, you'll also more efficiently build stronger relationships with your contacts. Who doesn't want to come back to another awesome party?

The most important factor to consider is preparation; you can't just assume you're going to throw a great shindig without taking the time to set it up. Consider this your pre-party checklist:

- Make sure you have a variety of food and drinks available and keep in mind that not everyone likes alcohol. Ideally look to provide a combination of healthy snacks and junk food so all of your guests are happy.

- Keep music flowing throughout the party - get a stereo setup, play iTunes on your computer, or utilize your TV. The type of music you play doesn't matter too much as long as you have *something* playing (the worst type of music you can play is no music).

- Get at least three or four activities going your guests can enjoy – this ensures your friends have the opportunity to have fun and mix it up when they don't feel like chatting.

- Develop a solid movie library so that you have entertainment available during the waning hours of the night.

- Have a friend or two help you prepare for the party — whether it be cleaning up, purchasing food, setting up games/activities, or contacting friends.

- Be sure to lock your valuables away before the party so you won't have to worry about things being stolen.

When the party starts, take a deep breath and just look to have fun. If you focus on ensuring everyone has a good time while keeping guests safe, you'll be fine.

4) Joining Clubs or Teams

Joining a few different clubs or sports teams in your area is an excellent way to increase your social circle. When you can get into a steady rhythm of meeting somewhere at least once a week, you build lasting friendships easily. Seeing this group with consistency will naturally lead to great relationships.

The more areas you know about or are interested in, the more people you will feel comfortable around. So be looking to stretch your comfort zone by checking out a variety of groups. Like I discussed earlier with The Four Personalities, you want to have a well-rounded life. Maintaining a healthy mix of people you hang out with and activities you partake in all but guarantee a great balance.

Make sure to join clubs and teams that hold you accountable; there should be consequences for missing a meeting or game. This makes you value your time together and take the gatherings more seriously. You don't want to be a part of something where you just see one another when you all feel like it. A solid structure based on commitment helps foster your relationships.

Again, utilize the website http://meetup.com to locate clubs or teams close to you. If you're specifically looking to join a sports team, you can always check your local gym for leagues and sign up for a roster spot there.

5) Meeting Strangers

Keep in mind that you have hundreds of opportunities throughout the week to meet new people you don't know. In line at Starbucks, picking up dry cleaning, going out for a jog, finding a book at Barnes and Noble, etc. - no matter where you are, you are constantly surrounded by potential friends.

Strike up some small talk, find a few things in common, and then ask to exchange contact information. Even though everyone is usually very busy, we all appreciate a friendly but brief chat from time to time. Most people would love to make new friends but simply lack the courage to speak up – so be the person who engages the world. If you get into the habit of doing this a few times a day, you can meet well over a thousand people a year.

 Your Game Plan For Meeting People (Part 2)

Now that you have a few solid options for *where* to meet people, let's discuss *how* to best move these relationships forward. Ideally you want to be very comfortable meeting three types of people: potential friends, potential romantic partners, and potential business associates. Before we tackle each of these areas, I want to set some ground rules for you.

When you meet someone for the first time, he or she is going to respond completely differently to you based on your demeanor. They are waiting for your personality to set the stage for the interaction and will behave in alignment with that. For instance, if you are approaching someone for the first time with an apologetic tone like, "Sorry to bother you, but I was wondering..." you set them up to behave with authority over you. They might even start thinking, "Yeah, you are kind of bothering me" because of how you set the stage.

Back when I was in sales years ago, I was constantly looking for new customers every chance I could. Before I knew any better, I used to approach people and say, "Hey I don't want to bother you, but I have something that you might think is pretty cool. Don't worry, I'm not trying to sell you anything." Most of the time I received horrifying grimaces and desperate attempts to look the other way. When someone finally told me, "You *are* bothering me and it's *obvious* you're trying to sell me something," I quickly learned my lesson.

The lesson is to always assume a strong demeanor that expects both you and the person you're talking with to enjoy the interaction. Don't point out any potential concerns of the exchange going poorly; the other person will easily seize authority over you. It's not that they are judging you or are being cruel – it's simply how you set the stage. Rather than being apologetic and weak when you introduce yourself, be assertive and optimistic and the world will treat you with respect.

As a good rule of thumb, always expect people you don't know to treat you well and enjoy your company. Even if someone's body language is non-receptive and they don't seem to be responding to you, just assume they like you. More often than not, you will see your self-fulfilling prophecy take shape - people will respond to you favorably because you're thinking the best of them. Watch how they open up to you when you expect them to play the role of Mr. Nice Guy.

As you sharpen your skills for developing relationships, always keep in mind, "What do I really want the other person to feel after meeting me?" - and keep your demeanor in line with it without questioning whether or not they're going to follow suit.

Meeting Potential Friends

Friendship happens naturally over the course of time between two people. There's usually a give and take that goes on; he might do a small favor for you, then you might return the favor, and then you become friends. Or you might discover you have several things in common over the course of time that leads to you hanging out more often. These relationships move forward pretty easily.

However, to fully maximize the bond you have with potential friends, it's vital to implement a *little extra* attention. This additional amount of focus will elevate the connection you have with new contacts to another level and can also be applied to your current peer group.

For starters, flex as much of your full personality as possible when meeting a potential friend for the first time. Most of us do exactly the opposite – we show up at about 50% to avoid being outright rejected. We tend to tread water lightly, throwing out jokes and unique ideas slowly over time in careful doses. But if you simply show as much of who you are as possible when you first meet, you'll find commonalities faster, be more comfortable around each other, and will know if he or she is someone you want to have in your life almost immediately.

Ask yourself this – would you rather have someone get to know and appreciate the "safe" and "boring" side of you first and then later criticize your other half or immediately recognize your personalities don't mix up front and save both of you the time?

By the same token, consider encouraging your new acquaintances to comfortably show you their full personality up front as well. The more you let your guard down and just relax around someone new, the more inspired they will be to showcase exactly who they are. This is extremely beneficial to you because if you *don't* enjoy their personality, you won't have to waste any effort building a relationship that's headed nowhere – and if you *do* appreciate who they are, your friendship will grow much faster.

Here are three keys to building strong friendships:

1) Practice Acceptance

Give new acquaintances the space to express who they are without judgment. If they say something off-putting or out of place while you're getting to know one another, be cool with it. You kill any chance at forward progress if you try to shoot down something that goes against your beliefs during the first few moments of conversation. This initial time with both of you trying to get to know one another is fragile; there's simply not enough invested in the relationship for it to continue with much disagreement.

This doesn't mean you should tolerate *everything* someone tells you. Instead, incorporate an opposing belief threshold: if someone shares a few beliefs or opinions that contradict what you personally think is true, let them slide at first. Give the relationship "wiggle room" so that you can maintain different viewpoints without having to butt heads. However, once the threshold is exceeded – either too many opposing beliefs are present or something is said that clearly violates one of your core values – walk away.

Practicing acceptance with a person means avoiding the need to control or change their core personality. You can certainly assist someone in gaining a new perspective, but ultimately, their beliefs won't be dramatically shifted. For this reason, it's best to either anticipate a few conflicting thoughts here and there and just let them slide or simply stop spending energy on your friendship altogether. Any choice in the middle of this spectrum creates a gray area between you that can be annoying to navigate through.

2) Do More than Expected

If you have the potential to do a favor for someone, go slightly beyond what they would ask for or expect – and do this *without expecting anything in return.* The key difference between a high quality and low quality friend is this: they are willing to go the extra mile without assuming they will be immediately compensated. They give value freely and often and don't worry about getting their "fair share."

No matter how small, surprising a person with something extra they were not anticipating always bolsters your friendship because it's RARE. Very few people think like this – it's usually W.A.M. (what about me) or W.H.Y.D.F.M.L. (what have you done for me lately).

So the next time you're hanging out with a new friend, pay for their coffee, help them out with a project they're involved in, drive them somewhere they need to be, or pass on a movie or book you think they would like. Just doing a little bit extra without expecting anything in return will strongly motivate someone to have your back when it matters most.

Keep in mind that people tend to avoid asking others for help or support because they don't want to impose. So be in tune with ways you can help another person out without them needing to even ask you. You don't even need to offer much time and energy; small unexpected support here and there adds up to a profound difference. Pay particular attention to any areas they seem stressed out about and take five minutes to alleviate some of their anxiety. For example, if a buddy tells you he's been stressed out about his workload, throw him a book recommendation for time management, an article you found online about productivity, or a technique you've personally utilized that worked for you.

By taking quick action to provide solutions for your friends' problems, you show them you actually care about what they're dealing with. This is far more valuable than simply listening to someone vent their frustrations and saying, "yeah that sucks." By having a wide variety of simple but effective resources available in your back pocket, you automatically become a more appreciated friend.

I have a friend I always look forward to sharing time with because of this very reason: he consistently recommends new resources for me every time we talk. I can ask him for some additional information in a thousand different subjects and he always has a book, audiotape, video, movie, article, or program ready to suggest. You certainly don't have to take your knowledge this far, but even knowing a few effective resources in these key areas will make you a more appreciated connection:

- Productivity and Time Management

- Health (specifically weight loss)

- Relationships

- Money, Marketing, or Sales

Here's what I suggest doing as soon as possible: find as much valuable information as you can in the four aforementioned subjects. Then make a list of your top five resources in each topic. They don't have to be anything elaborate or complex; even a simple article or video you found online can be extremely helpful. Have these ready to go and test them out whenever you get a sense that someone wants to learn more about something or is struggling in a key area.

Bring up your recommendation casually without being too pushy – using the workload stress example from before, you can say something like, "Oh yeah that used to drive me crazy. I found a good book about it on Amazon a few months ago that helped me get more productive in the office. You should check it out." If they fight back or question it, then just drop it altogether – not everything you put out there is going to be embraced.

On the flip side, any time you receive value from one of your friends, express as much gratitude as you can. Go above and beyond to thank them for any level of support they give you. While most of us are unaccustomed to others reaching out to help us, we are even more unaccustomed to hearing someone express true heartfelt gratitude for us. If your buddy buys an extra ticket to a sports game and takes you with him, give him a call the next day saying how much fun you had and how thankful you were he took you along. At the very least send him a text message and let him know you enjoyed the experience. Most of us take these personal connections for granted and they can erode a friendship.

3) Show Them Why They're Valuable

Remember that we all want to feel powerful, loved, wise, and valuable. These are the four identities that most contribute to happiness and high self-esteem. When you do the little things that show you believe your new friend is valuable, he or she will think of you as a consistent source of happiness in their life.

First and foremost, be extremely considerate of their time. Don't keep a person waiting around without notice or run more than fifteen minutes late for your meetings. Being sloppy with these commitments is one of the most destructive things you can do for a relationship. Think about how you feel when someone leaves you waiting around – frustrated, bored, confused, and unappreciated are some of the emotions that come to mind. While it's easy to forgive someone for running late, we don't easily forget it – so respect your friend's time the same way you do your own.

Take a few extra seconds to also introduce them to your friends at social gatherings. Don't be the guy who cuts a conversation abruptly short to catch up with someone else while leaving his friend just standing there. Whenever someone else barges in, make it a point to quickly introduce him to whom you were just talking. This way everyone feels incorporated and no one gets left standing twiddling his thumbs.

In addition, remember some details about their life and bring them up in conversation. Show that you care enough about your friends to be paying attention to their hobbies, family, goals, job, and interests. As a quick and easy example, ask a person what his or her favorite type of cocktail is. Then the next time you meet up for a few drinks, order it for them. Or, if alcohol isn't your style, ask them about what they do at work. Say something like, "I was curious to find out what exactly you do there – what are you working on now?" As soon as they mention a small project or idea they're looking to accomplish, take a mental note. The next time you see one another, ask them about its progress by bringing up its SPECIFIC name. The fact that you remembered exactly what they have been spending their time on is far better than asking, "So how's that thing you're doing going?"

There are plenty of ways you can show a friend that they're valuable. By simply applying a little more concentration and effort into the relationship, most people will immediately feel more appreciated. However, as you apply this to your life, make sure you don't do any of these things to be compensated for your own needs. Everything you do for someone must stem from your desire to help and support them – NOT in order to get something from them. If you ever feel like you're trying to buy someone's friendship, you're headed in the wrong direction.

Meeting in the Business World

Your goal in networking events is to meet as many people as possible you feel will be a strong resource for you in business. Whether they are a potential client, business partner, alliance, or team member, you want to create a lasting impression and you want them to remember who you are when you call. The key to achieving this is by providing value as quickly as possible and by also showing that you have access to a lot of resources. Keep these two questions in mind to ask people:

1. What's your biggest challenge right now in your job/company?

2. What are you most excited about right now in your life?[15]

These questions come from Michael Ellsberg's book *The Education of Millionaires*. They're extremely powerful because they cut to the core of what most people are thinking about and looking to find solutions for. Rather than drone on about various topics they may or may not find compelling, you surgically slice right to the heart of their biggest interests. If you know what someone is struggling with, you're in a better position to help them – either with your own product or service or via referral. If you understand what someone is excited about, you immediately find out what they're passionate about and can keep them engaged with you as long as you like. These two questions not only make your new contact feel more comfortable engaging in conversation with you, they show that you know how to provide meaningful value.

To further stand out from everyone else in business, as soon as someone asks you how you're doing, stop saying, "I'm fine" or "I'm OK." 99% of the world is "OK." I can't tell you how many people I meet when I ask this question give me the same lukewarm answer out of habit. Most of the time their entire personality is boring; the business card is boring, the business they represent is boring, and *they* are immensely boring. Be different and say *anything* else - amazing, delightful, persnickety, outstanding, fantastic – you get the picture.

When someone asks you what you do for a living, be ready to give a little more than simply a one-note response. For example, being someone who helps others make millions by properly managing their money is more interesting than being an accountant. Instead of telling someone you're in marketing, explain how you're an expert in utilizing psychology to influence buying behavior.

Creating a quick one or two sentence description of what you do and what you provide for the world helps distinguish you from the thousands of people who share your profession.

Once you're both clear on what the other does for a living, see how you can help one another out. Do you have potential referrals for his business? Does he know of someone that could be a potential client for you? Does one of you have knowledge or resources the other could benefit from? Keep these things in mind and be sure to get their business card so you can follow up with them later.

As you're milling about the venue meeting people, make it a point to be socially proactive. Very few people have the confidence to outright introduce themselves to you so get in the habit of initiating contact first. Any time you see someone standing alone who looks unoccupied, extend your hand for the firm handshake and introduce yourself. These people are typically more shy than others, so be prepared to carry the conversation – this is an excellent time to put what you've learned so far into practice.

If you ever find yourself with no one to talk to, just introduce yourself to a group of people who are already talking. Say something like, "Hey guys - I just wanted to introduce myself and say hello." Shake hands with everyone in the group and exchange greetings - then isolate one person by pulling him or her aside. When you do this, ask them a quick follow-up question about what they do for a living, how they know the host of the event, or anything related to their business. By doing this, you ensure the group won't feel rudely interrupted by giving them the space to continue commiserating. (They will just have one less participant temporarily.)

Another potential awkward moment can arise if someone you don't know interrupts your conversation and no one has taken the proper steps to introduce you. If this happens, step right back into the conversation by introducing yourself with both your first *and* last name. This makes your presence known while politely emphasizing the fact that you were not properly introduced. If you do not do this, five minutes later you'll hear, "I'm sorry, I didn't catch your name. Who are you?"

Likewise, when you are in a position to introduce your contacts, do so as often as possible. Be constantly looking for opportunities to bring two people who don't know each other together. Any time two of your friends or associates end up in close proximity to one another and haven't had the opportunity to meet, introduce one to the other. When you do, take consideration to highly edify both of them. This means to introduce each one in a way that quickly highlights who they are and what they excel in. Your associates will truly appreciate it, feel like they know each other more comfortably, and experience a surge of confidence.

Make it a priority throughout each networking event to include as many people as you can into your conversations. Don't get into the habit of excluding people and brushing them off – you never know who could be a huge resource for you. Any time you notice someone behaving with shyness, help them out by pulling them into the discussion. Ask for their specific opinion or viewpoints and welcome any of their thoughts. Some of the most brilliant people are those who struggle the most in social situations!

Just remember to have fun while you respect the environment's atmosphere. While you shouldn't be unprofessional or overly casual, you don't have to be completely serious and mechanical. Often by being playful and light-hearted, you provide the breath of fresh air most people need throughout the whole night. Don't be afraid to show your personality and sense of humor.

Meeting Women

There are endless opportunities for you to meet members of the opposite sex around you daily. The mindset you need to adopt is that the world around you can and wants to be communicated with at all times. It's easy for us to fall into our own comfortable shell and mindlessly plow through the day, ignoring those we could potentially be meeting around us. If you open up to others on an ongoing basis, you'll be surprised how eager people are to make new friends.

Women, no matter how beautiful, are no different. They WANT you to have the courage to strike up conversations and they WANT you to do so with confidence in how you present yourself.

As long as you remain friendly and upbeat without being annoying, they will always welcome an introduction. So if you are single, always keep your radar up for opportunities to make small talk. Affirm this on a continuous basis: "Women everywhere are open and willing for me to meet them."

Because striking up conversation in this fashion can be daunting at first, here is a quick strategy for working up the nerve to smoothly reach out to women:

- For one week, practice making eye contact, smiling, and saying "hi" to everyone you pass by when you're out running errands.

- For the next week, make small talk with at least 10 people (either male or female)

- For the third week, ask at least 10 women a quick question (ask for the time, directions, the nearest store you're looking for, etc.)

- For the fourth week, compliment at least 10 women as you pass by them without expecting the conversation to continue

- For the fifth week, take the suggestions you're about to read and meet at least 10 women

I recommend building up your confidence in a gradual manner like this because it's easy to get discouraged if you try to dive into the deep end headfirst. If, however, you want to just GO for it, by all means – stretch yourself and look to meet as many women as possible. Just recognize that more important than getting immediate results is getting the practice under your belt. Your intention shouldn't be to set up a date with the first person you meet; rather, it should be to LEARN SOMETHING NEW each time and gather reference points for your brain. If you approach enough women in this fashion, the likelihood that the next one you meet becomes attracted to you will consistently increase over time.

All right, enough generalities. Let's get to the specifics.

Before I attempt to explain anything, I'm going to answer the million-dollar question you probably have on your mind right now: "What do I say to a woman at first when I meet her?" Do you want to know the answer?

Are you ready?

Are you sure?

I don't think you can handle this...

It's going to BLOW YOUR MIND...

This CHANGES EVERYTHING...

Ok...

Here goes...

Say something *boring*.

Huh? What? Not as jaw-droppingly brilliant as you had anticipated? The truth is, it really does not matter what you say. The ability for you to carry on a conversation and get into an easy flow with the woman is what matters. All you simply need to say is SOMETHING that gets the ball rolling.

Recall that body language and vocal tonality make up over 93% of our communication in most contexts. Rather than focusing on *what* to say, I suggest focusing on your body language and facial gestures. Be sure to SMILE, be LOUD (but not overbearing), and hold a STRONG POSTURE (shoulders back and chest out). Use a mixture of the Authoritative and Statement Tonalities to set the stage for the conversation and just look to have FUN.

Are you ready for some of my favorite "openers?" Here you go:

"Hey, what's up?"

"How's it going?"

Or my all time favorite...

"Hi."

If you come across a book that tells you to develop some witty pre-canned response to vomit out of you, throw it in the trash compactor. Honestly, you could even step on a woman's foot by mistake, and it's going to get you the same results as some lame "pick up line."

The important step in this process is what comes next. Naturally, if you're feeling a little nervous, you will tighten up and only be able to think of simple, trite things to talk about. Here is where you *don't* want to be boring. Whatever you do, do NOT slip into INTERVIEW MODE. This is when you play twenty questions with her by asking the same annoying questions everyone always asks when they meet someone. "So what do you do?" "Where do you live?" "How long have you been doing that?" "How long have you lived there?"

Don't sound like you belong behind a desk in a suit. Instead of asking these inane questions, make a comment about her. If she has something unique about her, such as a warm smile or great eyes, tell her. If you're genuinely attracted to her, tell her you think she's cute. Or make an assumption about her: "You look like an architect." Assumptions are powerful because they position you as the leader of the conversation. Even if you are totally off, you might make her laugh by how wrong you are, and if not, at least explain the answer you want to hear. You'll get her talking more than just feeding you one line, boring answers.

Throughout the conversation, stay away from being serious and keep up a playful vibe. David DeAngelo, author of the book *Double Your Dating,* calls this vibe "cocky and funny."[16] Cocky not in the sense that you're being arrogant or conceited, but cocky in the sense that you know at a core level you are a man of tremendous value and are not afraid to show it. The funny side comes out of you as you keep things light and playful throughout the interaction. I really can't stress this enough: DO NOT be overly SERIOUS!

Remember what we talked about earlier with Tension vs. Desire. Don't show your hand too early and fall head over heels for her. Even as you compliment her and tell her you think she's cute, use the authoritative tonality. Your mindset throughout the first conversation you have with a woman must be, 'Let's find out how genuinely cool and fun she is and if she can hang on my level.' It's not, '*OH MAN she's so HOT she's so HOT she's so* HOT!'

Once you get into the flow of a relaxed conversation, use command language to set up a potential date together. Your goal is to communicate that you're serious about seeing her again and you're confident you both will have a good time. Don't ask to get her phone number, instead TELL her to give it to you. Say something like, "Give me your number so we can stay in touch. I know a great coffee shop with amazing desserts – we'll meet up there." This way you show her you're a confident man in control of his life from the second you meet her.

Worst-case scenario, she politely declines or tells you she has a boyfriend. Even if you get an objection like this, be prepared to ask again. Here's why: women are asked out on a never-ending basis – they simply don't have the time or the resources to say yes to every single offer. They develop an easy barrier (usually subconsciously) to weed out weak guys by initially shooting down an invitation to hang out later. If you simply talk to her a bit longer, stay relaxed, and don't let it bother you, you can actually ask again without any problems. The fact that you have the confidence to ask her twice in and of itself will make a HUGE impact in her eyes.

If she's still adamant about not seeing you one on one, then respect her boundary. Instead, give her *your* number and tell her the next time she's hanging out with friends to let you know so you can bring yours. Your intention here is to not look to date her, but to meet her friends instead (who are potentially single and at the very least could lead to you meeting more women).

OK, again, I know what you're thinking, "This all sounds awesome, but what if I just get blatantly shot down?" Don't worry, I got you covered.

 **On Rejection**

Rejection stings and can gnaw at a man's psyche unless he begins to understand it more closely and then mentally reframe what's going on. If you gain enough awareness about this process and even embrace the idea of rejection, you'll be able to shrug it off with indifference when you face it. Recall that your brain is wired to handle it the same way it unconsciously handles physical pain – this awareness is the first critical step in gaining leverage.

Think back to a time recently (or as recently as possible) when you felt you were painfully rejected. Recall the event in your mind and put yourself back in the scenario. Imagine where you were, who you were with, and what was taking place at the time. Replay the event as best as you can a few times. Now take a second to shift your attention entirely OFF of yourself and onto the other party. What do you think the other person was feeling or thinking while they were rejecting you? What kind of emotional state were they communicating from? What do you think led them to this negative response?

Here's what you can take away from this exercise: notice that you probably didn't feel too great about stepping into the other person's shoes. Their emotional state and self-esteem more than likely felt weak and pretty low. The reason this is the case is because the more cruelly we treat other people, the worse we feel about ourselves. If someone treats you particularly poorly and without compassion, you can be assured they suffer from extremely low self-esteem. At the very least, they were going through a particularly rough day and didn't show enough willpower to hold back their anger.

We tend to treat others the way we treat ourselves. If you're full of confidence, self-respect, and appreciation, how often would you lash out at others? Never! You would naturally want to share your high self-esteem by helping people feel better about themselves. The only reason a person would ever disrespect another is because they don't respect **themself.**

Think about this the next time you are faced with a particularly cruel person. Instead of getting defensive, angry, or cowering away, simply tell them, "It must be hard going through whatever pain you're carrying with you. I hope you feel better tomorrow." The truth will shake them to the core.

Let's change gears and imagine someone turning you down in a more friendly, socially acceptable way. Perhaps you strike up a conversation with an attractive single woman, share a few jokes, and then ask for her phone number. She politely shakes her head and declines your request to see her again. In this instance, it certainly wouldn't be fair to assume she had low self-esteem (although she might). More than likely, you simply didn't feel comfortable around her or failed to act with confidence and authenticity. Don't worry; this is completely fixable.

A huge reason why men struggle with behaving confidently in situations where social rejection is possible is because the mind focuses on every word they speak and action they make with intense criticism. Instead of allowing themselves to simply behave as they would around a close friend, their mind seizes control of their behavior and severely restricts them. Remember, our brains are wired to tread carefully around social acceptance; it monitors what we communicate with a stricter standard to ensure we don't overly offend or anger someone else.

Let's take a look at the classic example of a guy on a date with a girl he finds very attractive. The more valuable and rare he deems her to be, the more pressure he puts on himself to showcase the best side of his personality. Every laugh that he earns will give him a boost of self-assurance while every odd look or awkward moment will send him plummeting. This is because he feels that "screwing up" and losing his chances to get with the woman would be very damaging; not only is he losing out on a very attractive person, he's also getting rejected by one. So how does he behave during the date? He tightens up, restricts his personality to one-fifth of who he really is, and behaves in a fake and robotic manner, which ultimately disgusts and/or bores the woman into never wanting to talk to him again.

If you allow your brain to completely stifle and slam the brakes on your personality, I can all but guarantee you won't make a favorable impression on someone. The solution to these types of situations has to come from a shift in perspective.

Flowing From Self-Consciousness to Self-Awareness

Have you ever considered the difference between these two concepts? Self-awareness is having a clear understanding of who you are – your strengths, weaknesses, thoughts, beliefs, emotions, and motivations behind why you do what you do. This allows you to see directly how your thoughts and emotions are affecting you and helps you understand other people and how they perceive you. Having a healthy amount of self-awareness means you can tell when someone else is getting bored by what you're saying or when they are enthralled with you.

Self-consciousness, on the other hand, is an acute sense of self-awareness and a preoccupation with oneself. This version of awareness is extremely SENSITIVE to slight details or impressions. A highly self-conscious person tends to think about himself TOO much during social interaction. For example, he tends to think things like, "I hope there's nothing in my teeth...that was stupid of me...I shouldn't have said that...I bet my hair looks ridiculous...they're all looking at me now."

The key difference between these two lies in BALANCE. Notice that self-awareness is the perception of you and your relationship with the environment. Self-consciousness is an overly obsessed version of self-awareness that is too concerned with oneself and not concerned enough with the outer environment.

If you catch yourself stifled or over-analyzing what you're communicating, you're being overly self-conscious. An easy way to correct this is to simply snap your focus onto your environment. Instead of thinking about yourself, pay attention to the people around you (who you're speaking to). Ask yourself, "I wonder what's going through her head...does she seem stressed out or relaxed...what is she self-conscious about right now?" By taking the mental spotlight off of yourself, you give your brain a new task and shift it out of "babysitting" mode. You can't be restricting the words that flow out of your mouth and focus on someone else simultaneously; the mind can only handle on one thing at a time.

By centering your thoughts on another person, your physiology literally changes. You're able to practice stronger body language because you will maintain stronger eye contact, your posture will loosen up and relax, and your face will actually make subtle alterations throughout the conversation that indicate you're giving attention to every word they are saying. This mental shift literally makes your body appear more attractive.

Your Personal Laboratory

Another shift in perspective comes from viewing the world as your own laboratory or gym instead of a stage with a harsh spotlight on you. If you stop yourself from judging every outcome you receive as "good" or "bad" you will immediately gain a strong sense of self-assurance. When you view every event in your life, no matter how serious you believe it is, as something you go through to receive feedback, you can never lose. Stop beating yourself up over disappointing outcomes and focus on what you can learn instead. Think about what you can take away from it and then move on without getting your emotions tangled up.

We tend to tie up a lot of our self-worth into our results, and any time we receive results we don't anticipate, we usually beat ourselves up without mercy. We think, "This result was BAD and because it's BAD, I don't deserve to be successful." This type of thinking kills a person's desire to grow and experience new things. It locks us into a small box where we feel safe from encountering rejection and failure.

Shift your perspective by seeing the world as a laboratory where you're simply experimenting with different techniques and actions. When you receive feedback you weren't looking for, take a few mental notes, make some corrections, and simply try again. There's no need to bring frustration, anger, or anxiety into the picture.

T. Harv Eker, author of *Secrets of the Millionaire Mind*, talks about framing the concept of failure and rejection the way an actor would in his Wealth and Wisdom audio series. When an actor flubs a line and the director yells, "CUT!" to shoot the scene again, it's known as a *mis*-take. The key is in what happens next – the actor doesn't throw his script to the ground, whining about what a loser he is and how he can't get anything right. He simply moves back into position, refocuses, and tries again for the next take.[17] So from now on, whenever you commit a mis-take, simply gather yourself and try again. No self-punishment necessary.

Making this mental reframe opens up doors to you socially - it's your golden key to any city you want access to. When you go into any social scenario, whether it be meeting an attractive woman for the first time, making a presentation in front of a crowd, or even performing your job, with the mindset of "let's see what kind of results I get and what I can learn here," you free yourself. As an added bonus, this Zen-like indifference to the way people respond to you, ironically, leads to you coming off extremely confident and finding rejection far less often.

Push the limits of what you think you can get away with as often as possible. Have more FUN in your life by not being so worried about how people will react to you. See everything around you as a sandbox for endless exploration, ready to be molded and constructed as you see fit. If you get rejected or take it too far, so what? Make a few corrections and then move onto the next one!

The Parameters of Rejection

The next shift you need to make regarding rejection is what you believe defines it. I'd be willing to bet you've never taken a second to think about this. After all, I don't imagine anyone on the planet enjoys thinking about rejection. But consider this: what you believe to be a person turning you down could be a totally different experience for someone else. There is no written rule in society about the circumstances necessary for you to feel rejected.

When you experience a social situation that doesn't go according to plan, your brain DECIDES whether or not to classify it as "rejection." The sense of alienation you feel with another person comes entirely from you. Throughout your life, you have unconsciously written your own rules for deciding when you've been shot down, what that means to you, and how you will react to it. Most people carry this programming with them unconsciously and never question it or choose to change it.

Well, guess what? It's time to make a few alterations.

From now on, any time someone does or says something that you think *might* mean they think poorly of you, assume it's simply a friendly challenge. Assume everyone appreciates who you are and *expect* others to enjoy your personality. When someone says something questionable, just laugh or smile – as if to say, "This is interesting." Even if you're *absolutely* sure you're being mocked or criticized, don't allow yourself to feel jilted. Accept that another person's opinion of you is largely out of your control – so don't worry about it.

You have the power to go through hundreds of formerly awkward interactions with ease if you simply move the conversation forward without hanging your head and giving up. As soon as you feel that tinge of rejection coming, reframe it immediately as a friendly challenge. Just keep talking as if you're entirely unaffected – like water off a duck's back. You can't read peoples' minds anyway – so don't anticipate them reacting to you poorly if you don't know what they're truly thinking. You never know – that disgusted look they shot you could be about something else entirely. Maybe they had a rough day, are exhausted, or had a poor experience personally with what you're talking about.

If and when a person flat-out shoots you down and you can't find a way to reframe it in a positive way, just politely excuse yourself and walk away. Rather than muscling your way through a conversation, save your energy for a better match. There are some personalities you just won't get along with, and there are countless people in the world who don't have much kindness in their hearts (as previously mentioned, they usually have extremely low self-esteem). None of these factors have anything to do you with you as a person – so shrug them off and move on.

This is a good opportunity to remind you to not attach your happiness to a person's acceptance of you. If you meet someone new - especially a woman you find attractive - don't start immediately daydreaming about the two of you being together and falling in love. This kind of emotional attachment creates an illusion you believe is real. If she decides to move on or turn you down at some point, if you're invested in being with her for your own happiness, the more intense the rejection you'll suffer from.

Even worse, you'll want to blame her for your pain. However, this type of suffering is created strictly from *your* need to have a specific person in your life. Without this attachment, there is no distress when a person moves on without you. Rather than blaming a person for rejecting you, just turn your focus off of them. If they have made a decision to not spend their energy thinking about you, why should you spend any of yours thinking about them? Accept that things didn't work out and go meet more people – there are thousands out there waiting to discover how valuable you are.

Intimidation Protocol

Men are naturally competitive and combative with one another; it's in our blood. This competitive nature comes out often when two guys meet for the first time without expecting to. One of the most common scenarios for this type of behavior is at bars or nightclubs when males are competing for the attention of a woman. An unconscious hostility can be expressed through body language to more overt attempts to "tool" one another by winning verbal sparring matches. It's kind of like our own version of a National Geographic documentary on two rams charging forward and slamming into each other's heads.

In these situations, most guys respond with a fight or flight instinct. Some believe it's a point of pride to defend their "manhood" and even invite a physical confrontation. For the others, they tend to back down immediately without standing their ground. However, neither option is particularly beneficial; fighting someone all but guarantees an end to your evening and backing down shows everyone you're not strong enough to stand up for yourself.

The best way to handle a situation where someone is attempting to intimidate you is to completely reframe how you think of that person. Rather than relying on your outdated survival instincts of fight or flight, disengage from "survival mode" altogether. Instead of participating in the intimidation battle, shrug it off the way you would an annoying younger brother. Your goal is to show both him and the people you're with that he is not a threat with your body language, choice of words, and tone of voice. No matter how physically big or imposing he may be, you must be completely NONREACTIVE and DISMISSIVE of everything he does. In this way, your mind views him not as a threat, but an annoyance.

Here's why this strategy is far more effective than trying to fight him, out-yell him, or hide from him: you will get *him* to back down without much effort on your part. In addition, you will demonstrate superior intellect and a much higher level of poise than he could possibly muster.

To successfully pull this off, you need to demonstrate control over your mental focus. When another guy steps into the picture in loud, crowded, social venues and attempts to intimidate you, your brain wants to instinctively focus all of your attention on him. It fires up the fight or flight script and demands that you devote your inner resources entirely to him. This is not good; he owns your attention and everything he says or does has a high chance of making you to react to him - which is exactly what he wants.

Instead of letting your brain run on autopilot, direct your focus elsewhere and TUNE HIM OUT. The easiest way to do this is to simply ignore what he says and focus on whom you'd rather be talking to. If you're flirting with a woman you've just met and get interrupted by a guy like this, snap your attention directly back to *her* and continue talking. Have her lean close to you so only both of you can hear, and then talk about him as if he wasn't right in front of you. Say something like, "I'm really sorry about all of this – he just escaped from the zoo and is looking for a new home. I think if you stay perfectly still, he won't start humping your leg." Referring to him in a humorous context such as this will get her laughing and also thinking about him in a diminutive fashion. If being funny isn't your thing, just lean in and ask her, "Who's this creepy guy? What do you think he wants?" Regardless of what you say, he now has to interrupt both of you again to get your attention.

While you verbally ignore him, remember the lessons you took away from chapter four and refrain from giving him proper body language. Turn your torso AWAY from him so that you don't face him. Once again, you're subtly showing that you don't feel like he's a threat to you, which diminishes him in everyone else's eyes. If you want to take it a step farther, gently guide your conversation partner away from him with you, so that *both* of you now have your back to him. Making this simple move shows everyone you don't consider him important enough to even think about and broadcasts a powerful message deep into his subconscious that he is not going to be able to get to you.

The harder he tries to get your attention with you ignoring him, the more foolish he looks as you're engaging the people around you. If at this point you're still afraid of not "giving respect" to guys twice your size, let me explain this to you: unless you're hitting on his wife or have been hostile with him, he has no right to get physical with you. If you've been shutting him out and he does try to battle you, he will be seen in a very low light by everyone else. As long as you stay calm and refuse to engage him, every attempt he makes at getting your attention will come across as increasingly pathetic.

The biggest mistake you can make is to give him an inch and respond to an insult he hurls your way. Don't lose grasp of your game plan and let your ego take control of your emotions. As soon as you throw negative attacks *his* way, you've lost. I don't care how scathing they sound, you're playing a game you're not going to win. You're choosing the battle with him over winning new friends and having a good time, which won't endear you to anyone.

Okay, but what about the guys you can't really ignore – maybe it's just not socially acceptable or the guy is already friends with the new group or person you're talking to. Perhaps completely shutting him out just isn't feasible. If you absolutely must engage the guy, the key is to be playful and short with him.

The context you want to establish is that you're having a good time and being playful at your intimidator's expense. In doing this, you want your sentences to be short and to the point – the more you talk to him, the more attention you're giving him. Responding to whatever he says with something like, "cool, man" is a simple strategy for accomplishing this. For example:

He says, "Look at you, trying to impress these girls – could you be any more of a loser? What kind of game are you working with anyways? Look at what you're wearing! That shirt would be something I wore in middle school because I didn't know any better."

You say, "Right on, man." Then turn your back to him.

Regardless of what you say, remember that your objective is to only give him attention and acknowledgment when you absolutely need to. As soon as you're done speaking, you don't have to even face him to hear what he has to say in response. Continue your conversation with whomever you were speaking to as if he isn't there.

Framing

Framing is adding context to another person (usually humorous) that casts him or her in a less than desirable light. It's a potent weapon to have in your arsenal that you can use on someone particularly annoying. As a warning, I don't recommend framing a person unless everyone knows it's entirely playful or if the person has just been acting like an absolute idiot. This is a quick and effective method of burying someone if you know what you're doing. Here are some examples of what I'm talking about.

- Tired - "Hey man, are you okay? You look exhausted."

- Sick - "Everything okay, buddy? You don't look so good...you have these really dark circles under your eyes..."

- Try-Hard - "Hey man, don't try so hard. It's okay man, just be yourself."

- Stressed Out - "You all right? You seem stressed out. Something bothering you?"

- Defensive - "Calm down, Officer Sensitive. Relax. Don't get all defensive on me."

Framing someone is powerful because the recipient faces a lose-lose. If they don't say anything in response, it's assumed that they're accepting the new context and not denying it. Because you just painted them in a not-so-desiring light, this is not a good move. On the other hand, if they try to deny the context, they're reacting to you and losing ground by the second. You can experiment with different frames and get as creative as you want to. Generally painting an unfriendly and/or arrogant person as weird or creepy casts them out quickly and efficiently.

So what do you do when someone is attempting to throw a frame on *you*? Think of it as a lasso someone is trying to throw around your neck. If you struggle against it, the loop gets tighter around your neck. If you just stand there and pretend like it's not there, the guy can drag you around as much as he wants. So they key isn't to think about whether or not to ignore the frame – the key is in *how* you respond to the lasso around your neck. To maintain your swagger, you have to stay cool and calm in these types of situations while most people get defensive or angry.

There are a few ways to handle this. First, you can always simply laugh off what the person is saying and use dominant body language by placing a hand on the guy's shoulder to show you're not affected. It really doesn't matter what you respond with (or if you respond at all) if you're laughing and seemingly unaffected. You're also subtly using reverse psychology here; by laughing you're welcoming more attempts from him to try to get to you, but in his eyes, you seem to be enjoying it, so why should he bother?

Another trick is to replace his frame with a new, larger frame. So for example, if the guy has just asked you, "Hey dude, are you still living at home with your mom? Life must suck for you since dropped out of fifth grade." Instead of trying to defend yourself or throw out a come-back on the spot, build a larger frame: "Okay, I know you're trying really hard right now to be funny, but next time, I want you to let it come more naturally to you. Don't think about it so much." As soon as you throw out the new context, turn your back on him and don't give him the space to respond. You're not directly referencing his frame by responding to what's been said; instead, you're building a larger frame to push his out. How is he going to respond to that? "No, remember, I was talking about you staying at home with your mom..." Your back is already turned and he's out of options.

Lastly, you can "kill" him with kindness by just responding with something like, "Hey, man, you're better than that. Everyone here thinks you're a cool guy, right buddy?" Again, as you're saying it, pat him on the back or grab his shoulder for dominance. Then, turn your back on him and shut him out from any potential response.

Remember that it really doesn't matter what you say as long as you're not being overly serious or reactive. As long as you show that you're having a good time and unaffected by everything the guy trying to intimidate you is saying, you're going to be fine. These social strategies should only be used when all else has failed and you need to quickly bury the guy. You don't need to attack, you don't need to retreat – you just need to stand your ground.

Be "Un-Offendable"

It's a well-known psychological fact that people with the lowest self-esteem are offended the easiest. Another thing to keep in mind is that you only take offense to the things you find true on some level. If you're six foot eight and I were to try and insult you by calling you a midget, how would you respond? You'd probably laugh it off and think I was ridiculous. So let me ask you this: what's the difference between that and someone insulting your personality? If someone belittles you or tries to intimidate you, why would you respond with anything other than laughter?

In your eyes, you need to value yourself so highly that anyone attempting to chip away at your resolve is engaging in pointless behavior. If you take offense to someone attacking you, it means that you think what they are saying is true on some level. Manage your mood at all times and never let your emotions get out of hand because someone is trying to come after you. You don't have to get defensive or attempt to attack the person. Just smile and laugh and picture the guy trying to intimidate you as a tiny squirrel running circles around you while he tries to get your attention.

Your relationship with society mirrors the relationship you have with yourself. The more you value yourself, treat yourself with respect, and consider yourself a rare commodity, the less you will react to someone challenging you. The crux of mastering this boils down to the understanding of your own thoughts and emotions and how to utilize both to your advantage. If you can grasp a few more powerful ideas, you will truly be an "un-offendable" person.

Onto part three...

PART THREE:
THE UNSHAKABLE

Become the rock that cannot be moved.

7

EMOTIONAL STATE MASTERY

"People who learn to control inner experience will be able to determine the quality of their lives." – Mihaly Csikszentmihalyi

Time to change gears again. We just spent chapters four through six covering the outer mechanics of behaving with swagger and projecting authentic confidence. You now know how to talk, move, think, and carry yourself to attract others to you. The skills and strategies covered in these chapters will definitely help you navigate a variety of environments, and if routinely practiced, will allow you to handle most circumstances thrown your way. However, to truly comprehend this information on a core level, we need to look deeper. We're going to need to zoom into your inner world and examine the very roots of confidence.

You can think of part one as the foundation to the skyscraper you are building. You reinforced it by stripping away much of the weaknesses that were harming the integrity of the structure and replaced them with stronger support systems. Part two was about developing the building – adding the components that make the architecture look and feel the way you want it to. How tall the skyscraper ends up will boil down to how many concepts you apply into your daily actions and behaviors.

You can consider part three as your efforts to disaster-proof your structure – strengthening it so much that it can withstand hurricanes, earthquakes, tornadoes, and tsunamis. To effectively do this, it may be helpful to imagine your building as a living, breathing thing – perhaps a giant sequoia tree that doesn't flinch when faced with a variety of outer conditions. These next few chapters all concern extending the roots of your structure deep into the earth, allowing you to become absolutely unshakable.

The first task in beginning to get the knack of your inner world lies in understanding your emotions and the impact they have on your confidence. Whereas most people believe they have little to no control over their emotions and react to the world unconsciously, you're going to start developing a high level of internal awareness. You're going to master your emotional state and utilize this power to affect those around you in an unforgettable way.

In this chapter, you'll learn:

- What your emotional state is and how it affects your confidence

- How to assume complete responsibility for your emotions in order to consistently feel unshakable and strong

- How to affect an entire room's energy and become the life of the party

- Three tools for maintaining a powerful emotional state in any circumstance

Emotional State Awareness

Your emotional state is the culmination of how you're feeling in the present moment - for better or worse. When you have a STRONG STATE, you feel happy, joyous, excited, relaxed, at peace, inspired, motivated, or intrigued. When you have a WEAK STATE, you feel bored, saddened, angry, intimidated, shy, nervous, or alienated.

When you are in a weak state, it is impossible to feel confident and project swagger. You can't look cool if you're angry, suave if you're bored, or assured if you're sad. You could spend your entire life reading everything there is to know about confidence but none of it will matter if you are continuously in poor moods.

Most of you reading this book probably don't feel awful or depressed very often – it's probably something that comes once in a while and passes. I would guess that most of you feel OK or FINE most of the time. But here's the key point - just being OK or FINE doesn't do nearly enough to give you unflinching confidence. What makes the biggest difference is your ability to get yourself into a peak state and maintain it throughout the day.

There is a sea of difference between feeling fine and feeling incredible. Ask anyone how they're doing when you meet them and 99% of the time they're "good" or "OK" or "all right." A few months ago I was at the bank and overhead a grumbling old man walk in and explain to the teller he was "a shade over mediocre" - like he was a color or something. There are very few people who actually feel great in the world. (And for the record, I'm not talking about the Pollyanna people who plaster a fake smile to their face and pretend to be happy while quietly suffering.)

The key to taking your life to the next level lies in grasping this: you can't always control outer circumstances – but you can always control your inner world. You always have the power to choose how you want to feel. This power is extremely magnetic; people always want to be in the places where others are having a good time. If you can be the source of good emotions continuously throughout each day, you're going to be noticed and appreciated.

Fortunately, this is a skill you can improve with awareness and conscious effort if you take responsibility for your emotions.

Mind the Gap

Your emotions are always driving your behaviors and influencing your actions in each moment. When someone or something in the outside world bothers you, you usually react with a drop in state. If someone cuts you off in traffic, you perceive the event, feel angry, and honk or yell at the driver seemingly automatically. Then when you get home, you drop your knife down the sink drain, lose sight of it, feel upset, and cuss at it for slipping out of your hand. One thing happens (cause) and then we react to it (effect). Pretty standard procedure, right?

Not necessarily. There is a gap you have been largely unaware of throughout your life. It's a TINY gap that exists between the events that happen around you and your reaction to them. This gap makes the difference between whether or not you allow yourself to feel confident and in control or lost and downtrodden.

Here's where the gap lies: when something happens to you, you have the ability to CHOOSE what it MEANS to you.

This is because nothing has meaning until your mind assigns it meaning.

This is one of the deepest and fundamentally important points of the book.

> **NOTHING HAS MEANING UNTIL YOUR MIND ASSIGNS IT MEANING**

You have the ability at any given moment to feel happy or miserable by deciding what you want something to mean. This is because truth and fact are completely different.

FACT is what objectively happened – there's no room for dispute.

TRUTH is what you perceive to be true – a judgment you make on the situation.

There is only ONE fact. There are THOUSANDS of potential truths. With every event in your life, no matter how big or small, you create your own truth. If someone cuts you off in traffic, you *could* interpret it as someone being discourteous or rude to you. Or you could interpret it as someone being in a rush and desperately needing to get to where he wants to go. You could even take it to be an excellent opportunity to work on developing patience. There is no one correct way to think about it – everything is up to you.

With this in mind, the meaning you assign a situation directly impacts how you react to it. If you interpret the guy cutting you off in traffic as him being rude to you, you're going to probably react by yelling and screaming. This emotional outburst then weakens your state and you feel worse off than you were. Likewise, if you choose something more empowering, you can react by taking a deep breath and simply smiling, elevating your mood and ability to enjoy the day.

Most people slog through life reacting to everything coming their way without considering that they have the ability to choose what to focus on. If you can train yourself to MIND THE GAP and become aware of when you tend to lean towards a disempowering interpretation, you have the opportunity to completely alter your life. You will be unwavering even when things aren't going your way and appear to be negative and disruptive in the outside world.

Think about a three year old toddler who is exploring his parent's living room by climbing the family couch. Let's say he slips and takes a tumble, bouncing off the cushions and then landing on the carpet. He's not *really* all that banged up, but he's got a worried look on his face as he tries to make eye contact with his mother. Mom looks terrified, rushes over to make sure he's not seriously injured, and expresses genuine fear in her voice. How does the little guy respond? Typically by suddenly bursting into tears - when he sees Mom worried, he *decides* to start crying.

We're no different as adults. Falling off the couch can represent screwing up the major portion of a speech, forgetting something important at home, bombing a job interview, or otherwise humiliating ourselves in public. Once the moment passes, we decide whether or not we will start "crying" based on what we choose to make it mean.

Recognize the gap throughout the day – consistently seek opportunities to re-evaluate what potentially negative events could mean. Before you unconsciously react to what's happening, take a few deep breaths and relax. Allow a variety of interpretations to flood into your brain and choose the one that supports you the most. Ask yourself, "how does this help me?" and "what kind of person do I have to be to rise above this?"

For example, if you're frequently aggravated at work, assign empowering meanings to what people say to you more often. If your boss upsets you, shift the context. Ask yourself, "How does this make me a better person?" Or, "How can I feel thankful to learn this?" Reframe the entire episode in your mind until you are free to carry out the rest of your day without feeling angry. This way, you select powerful responses that uplift your emotional state instead of destroying it.

If you're thinking, "Yeah but negative things happen that are out of my control all the time – how do I not let them get to me?" consider the life of Viktor Frankl. Frankl suffered through the Holocaust and had to see his wife, father, mother, and brother die in the concentration camps of Nazi Germany. While enduring hunger, frozen temperatures, brutality, and the constant threat of death, Viktor had every opportunity to consider life meaningless and suicide a reasonable choice. Yet somehow he emerged from the darkest period of not only his own life, but also millions throughout the world, as a staunch optimist. Frankl went on to write *Man's Search for Meaning*, his masterpiece on the human spirit and the power of cultivating a life purpose.

In the book, Frankl writes, "The one thing you can't take away from me is the way I choose to respond to what you do to me. The last of one's freedoms is to choose one's attitude in any given circumstance."[18]

If Viktor found the inner strength to develop this mentality during perhaps the most devastating period of human existence, what excuse do you have?

It's easy to play the role of the victim when we encounter frustrating moments. It's easy to focus on the cruelty of others and our own misfortunes when we endure tough times. Our conditioned minds would much rather lash out at the world instead of assume responsibility for the way we feel. This is because taking responsibility means giving up the chance to play the "poor me" card. However, this mindset is not only detrimental to your happiness – it eats away at your confidence like a virus.

A surefire recipe for being a weak, pathetic person is to shrug off accountability for your thoughts and emotions. You'll feel as if you have very little control over your life and ability to influence change. However, the more diligently you manage the meanings you take away from your experiences, the stronger your inner fortitude becomes. Your backbone gets reinforced every time you reframe a potential setback as a beneficial understanding.

Whatever happens to you during your time on Earth, no matter how seemingly terrible, you must accept complete responsibility for your attitude. Just remember that you are in constant control of how you feel in any given situation – no matter how rough, annoying, boring, or desperate reality seems. You're still the little kid who is about to decide whether or not he wants to start crying or shrug it off and bounce back up.

Moving from Temporary to Permanent State

Without question, you have already experienced several moments in your life that left you feeling great about yourself. When the stars align and certain circumstances fall into place, you're going to access an empowering emotional state. Naturally, there are several factors that usually do this for you. They are:

- Dressing well

- Being around good friends

- Your competency in a given situation

157

- How familiar you are with a place/situation

- Your role/level of leadership in a given environment

- Voluntarily stretching yourself to the limit physically or mentally

Think about those moments in your life when you felt confident because you wore a new outfit you thought looked cool. Or the time when you did something completely outside of your comfort zone and felt proud of yourself. Or, if you're an athlete, any time you gave it your all during the final seconds to win the game. These moments are fantastic ways to feel strong and access a higher state.

However, none of them last forever. Your clothes stop feeling crisp and new after a few months. You lose the next game in a tight battle and feel demoralized. You find yourself in a new situation you're unfamiliar with and recognize no one there. Where did your confidence go?

I'm positive you bought this book because you no longer want to depend on these temporary moments as your only opportunities to feel great. Again, I'm not advocating for you to ignore them – in fact, you should look for as many ways to experience them as possible. However, if you want to possess unconditional confidence that sticks with you in a variety of circumstances, you need to develop the skill of generating confident emotions internally. You won't always be able to control the situations you find yourself in. But you can always sharpen your awareness of what makes you feel strong and at ease.

Society tends to believe that what you have, do, look like, or know should dictate your confidence. Most think that a person's extrinsic reality is responsible for eliciting his or her emotions. I agree to a point; it's clearly difficult to feel annoyed when we receive an unexpected gift of money or excited to find a flat tire. However, I believe most people overlook the most important component of the recipe. They tend to focus so much effort on these temporary OUTER conditions that they completely miss the INNER conditions. Keep in mind Unshakable Swagger doesn't come from

WHAT you DO or HAVE – it comes from WHO YOU ARE. It's a state of BEING.

There are two areas of emotional expertise you can develop to raise this state of being: gratitude and fun. Gratitude, you'll notice, isn't something you can do or an outer event you can touch. It's an entirely internal feeling generated from within. While certain experiences can influence the level of gratitude you feel, you alone determine the depth of this emotion. Likewise, the concept of "having fun" is not found in the outer world. While certain activities are objectively more "fun" than others, only you can choose how enjoyable they are for you. Both of these emotions are entirely under your direction.

Let's take a closer look at having fun. First of all, generating this emotion is a SKILL and a HABIT that needs attention and requires mental effort. Most of us are terrible at it; our society has been trained to believe that having fun is wrong past a certain age and that we should be working instead. So how do we spend our free time? Vegetating in front of a television set – hey, if we're not supposed to have fun, we shouldn't be doing anything, right?

Seldom do we look to create entertaining experiences for ourselves; our reliance on TV and technology has rendered most of us extremely passive. If we're not immediately stimulated by something close by, we tend to feel bored and anxious. This means that we focus on what or who is entertaining *us* rather than generating our *own* fun. We place the responsibility of being "fun" into the hands of reality television stars, Facebook updates, and Youtube videos.

Let's get something clear: I'm not advocating that you shut off technology altogether and become some kind of pre-technological monk. What I *am* saying is for you to be less dependent on it to bring about amusement into your life. Instead, be proactive about feeling excited and curious about your surroundings. Take on the responsibility of making every reality engaging and interesting. In any given situation, ask yourself, "What's cool about this? How can I make this fun?" See everything as something the universe has put in your life for you to enjoy and experience as new.

For example, picture yourself in line at the DMV – one of the least enjoyable places people visit. For most of us, the process is close to a nightmare; boredom, anxiety, and aggravation are just a few of the many emotions that come up. But try asking yourself, "How can I have a good time here?" Strike up conversations with people next to you in line, make a few jokes about the shared hatred of the DMV, or if you're getting a new license, take a goofy picture. Put your mind to work by concentrating only on ways you can find entertainment rather than on what you dislike about the environment. By reframing the entire scenario as an opportunity to have fun, you're more likely to have a good time.

Always keep your radar up for opportunities to create fun in brand new ways. Consider being more unpredictable by stepping outside of your ordinary routines. If you notice you ever fall into a rut of just going through the motions in life, do something different immediately. Take new routes home from work, visit restaurants you've never been to, write with your left hand for a day if you're right-handed (and vice versa), surprise a friend with an accent, joke around with the barista at your coffee shop, or spontaneously start dancing in a crowded mall. When you begin to realize that enjoying life is an art and a skill you must nurture, you'll see possibilities everywhere for creating new experiences.

Most of us stick to a predictable routine because we know the odds of being rejected, mocked, or questioned are very low. However, being predictable will not only make *you* jaded with life, your friends and associates will feel bored with being around you as well. If you want to be forgotten most everywhere you go and bring few memorable experiences home with you, fly under the radar as often as possible. However, if you want to be a more exciting person with a long list of friends who love hanging out with you, be willing to do things society doesn't expect from you. Be willing to receive confused looks, shrugged shoulders, and snide remarks - and be OK with them. In fact, your threshold for dealing with awkward circumstances will directly affect how much fun you can end up having.

Once you begin infusing more fun into your life, practice the art of gratitude by paying attention to the things that you like or appreciate. If you do this consistently, you will find yourself in a

160

peak state because gratitude is one of the most empowering emotions you can maintain. The deeper you feel grateful for your current circumstances and the longer you hold this energy, the better you will feel in every aspect of your life.

You're going to have to exert more mental energy than you are used to in order to maximize this emotion. Our minds are simply not wired to look for things we're thankful for – they'd much rather concentrate on our problems, issues, dilemmas, and pains. Many of my clients whom I speak to about gratitude say something like, "I'll feel grateful when I finally get what I want in my life." This mindset is like chasing a dangling carrot while running on a treadmill; even if you get what you want, your mind isn't going to want to feel grateful for it – it's going to locate the next carrot to run after instead.

Begin training your mind to stop chasing after the carrots and become more invested in the here and now. Take responsibility for seeing the world around you as a reflection for all the things you enjoy about life. No matter who you are, what you've been through, or what situation you find yourself in, there are always countless reasons to feel grateful. If you can only think about reasons to complain, you're not thinking enough! Give your brain a workout and ask it to find ten reasons you're thankful for what you have – even when you don't feel like it.

Here's why this discipline will pay off for you: the more you're able to mentally locate reasons to feel grateful, the more reasons you'll have to access a strong emotional state. Remember that happiness and confidence work hand in hand; you truly can't experience one without the other. Even if you find yourself in a situation where you're confident while seemingly *not* feeling happy, on a subconscious level, you are finding enjoyment with what you are doing.

Begin applying this to your life immediately in every moment – no matter how big or small. When you're in a situation you would normally not care for, like being at the dentist' office, think about what you like about it. Ask your brain to find at least three things you enjoy about getting your teeth clean. Maybe you appreciate catching up with the receptionist, the music playing in the background, or even the way the place smells. Again, if nothing is coming to you, you're not stretching your mind enough – you have to make the effort to shift your focus.

The point here isn't to gloss over what you feel is bothering you – if there are circumstances you don't want hanging around, then focus on removing them. I don't suggest that you ignore what's hurting you by keeping your head in the clouds. However, every struggle possesses reasons for gratitude buried within. You're going to learn something new, appreciate something on a different level, or take on a different perspective with each new challenge. This mindset fortifies your spirit when handling unexpected problems; you'll start seeing how you can benefit from them while they occur.

The next time you face a predicament you didn't see coming, quickly ask yourself, "What do I enjoy about this right now? At the very least, what could I learn from this?" Your mind is going to give you answers based on the questions you ask it – so ask strong questions!

At the end of the day, what you can say thank you to is fuel for your life. The more you are truly thankful for, the more energized you will feel at work, school, or with friends. When you are grateful for what you have around you, it's hard to not have a smile on your face and assume a lighthearted demeanor. This easiness is highly attractive because you're broadcasting how awesome your life is to the world. Remember, most people are entirely caught up in their own drama, problems, and fears. Your relaxed attitude is going to be alarmingly refreshing - think about this the next time you're about to fire off a string of complaints.

If your current peer group is full of whiny complainers, take a good look at yourself – chances are that you're one of them. You have to make it a point to no longer condone this type of behavior – both from others and from yourself. The less you tolerate negativity and the more you emphasize gratitude, the more likely you are to find great friendships. In fact, the more grateful you are, the higher the caliber of people you meet. After all, if misery loves company, it stands to reason that happiness loves it too.

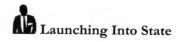 **Launching Into State**

I want to reinforce an important point I mentioned earlier in this chapter: it is your RESPONSIBILITY to influence your emotional state. Rather than going through your daily routine with a "let's hope something good happens today" mentality, you should be turbo-charging how you feel beforehand so that you're thinking three words: BRING IT ON.

There are two techniques you can utilize to launch yourself into a peak state so that you start each day at a high level. If you get into the habit of doing them consistently each morning, you will notice a night and day difference in how you feel. They are the key to taking the reins of your mind and steering it in the direction you want to go. In addition, any time you need a major boost of confidence, these strategies are your answer. Incorporate them into your life frequently and you will be far more prepared to handle events that used to frustrate and overwhelm you.

Visualization

The first technique is known simply as visualization. This is the process of imagining specific scenarios in your mind in which you're successful. You do this by closing your eyes and mentally seeing yourself obtaining what you want, behaving with poise, or having others react to you favorably. It's one of the most potent ways to elevate your self-concept because you're reconditioning your subconscious expectations.

What you visualize most will ultimately become your reality. Most of us experience this in a *negative* way; we tend to imagine our deepest fears coming true with painstaking detail. For example, if someone has recently rejected you, your brain probably played back a constant loop of the situation in your head. You visualize her shooting you down, giving you an odd glance, and turning her back and walking away over and over again with vivid recollection. Now how does that make you feel about wanting to go out and meet another woman? Awful. With this expectation, even if you do work up the courage to meet someone new, you're going to feel tense and awkward because of what you've been mentally rehearsing - it's all your mind believes is possible.

So instead of visualizing what already went wrong or what could go wrong, focus your thoughts specifically on what you want in the future. Play a ten to fifteen minute movie with you as the main character that sees you achieving exactly what you desire as if the event is happening now. If you're nervous about a major occasion, especially something you've never done before, this prepares your mind and body to behave in alignment with your desired outcome.

I used frequent visualization to prepare myself for the day I went skydiving. My biggest fear was taking the first step off the plane and beginning the free fall. I knew as long as I could work up the courage to take that major step, I'd be able to complete the dive. So for every day for three weeks, I took ten minutes to calmly see myself jumping out of that plane over and over again without hesitation. I looked at as many pictures and videos I could to create the airplane in my mind and played a short movie of me diving out of it endlessly. I imagined what I could see, hear, and feel around me as I jumped thousands of times. Because it felt so real and I was absolutely certain about the outcome I wanted, I was able to conquer my fear and experience one of the greatest moments of my life.

You can also use this technique to work on your self-concept. If there is any aspect of your personality you'd like to change or enhance, visualize yourself behaving in alignment. If you're normally a very shy person, picture scenarios where you are outspoken, extravagant, and bold. If you're the type of person who gets anxious easily, see yourself being calm, relaxed, and at ease with others. The more clear and thorough you are on the person you'd like to become, the more likely your mind will assist you in your transformation.

This process works because your brain cannot tell the difference between what is real and what is vividly imagined. By visualizing what you want to create, your subconscious is given crystal clear instructions for the specific reality you're intending to bring about. You're literally practicing having what you want.

Jerry Bergonzi, an accomplished jazz tenor saxophonist and composer, frequently utilizes visualization to his advantage. In his book, *Melodic Structures*, Bergonzi points this out: "With the use of visualization, the mind actually teaches the body and the mind remembers what the body is more apt to forget. The mind visualizes what the body does in multi-dimensional fashion. It practices the fingertips and the notes, it hears the sound and the content, it feels the intention, the emotion, and the nuances of what is played. The body then follows suit. The body teaching the mind is actually a backward process and for this reason through the use of visualization we are able to learn more quickly."[19]

Now let's be clear: I am no jazz tenor saxophonist, nor do I plan on ever learning how to become one. The reason this passage is powerful is because you can apply it to any and every aspect of your life. Struggling with speaking in front of large groups of people? Visualize yourself delivering an articulate speech, flowing through your sentences, and impacting the audience. Find it difficult to meet many people at networking events? Visualize yourself shaking hands with several people, exchanging business cards, and being introduced to everyone in the room. Single and challenged with finding a date? Visualize yourself starting conversations with women while you run errands, making them laugh, and getting some phone numbers.

Every minute you spend visualizing means it will take less trial and error to get the results you want. In fact, Bergonzi goes on to say, "Very often ten minutes of visualization is equivalent to two hours of physical practice." Imagine how much more unshakably confident you will feel before each day starts if you simply sit down and continuously imagine getting what you want. Your brain will become increasingly comfortable and familiar with helping you behave in alignment with what you want to achieve.

Keep in mind that the more energy and emotion you put into the process, the more you will get out of it. Our minds remember what we experience with emotional intensity – so the more vividly you see the success you want while FEELING as if you have it already, the more likely you are to step into that reality. If you can get into the daily habit of imagining and rehearsing what you want with

165

enthusiasm, you'll notice you start each day feeling better than you've ever felt before.

I recommend spending at least five to ten minutes doing this every morning before you begin your day. You will notice a HUGE difference in your confidence – I guarantee it.

Affirmations

Affirmations are simple statements you say out loud that reflect strong, positive beliefs about yourself. They're powerful because they work on both a conscious and subconscious level to rewire your own beliefs. By saying these declarations out loud, even if they don't represent your currently reality, your subconscious mind will begin accepting them as truth. With a stronger belief in yourself, you will take stronger actions - which lead to better results.

This is a particular area where feelings of unworthiness or self-doubt tend to show up. The more unworthy you believe you are, the more you will struggle with affirmations because your brain will be telling you these statements are not true. If what you're saying goes against how you think of yourself, your conditioned mind will react by telling you this is "stupid, pointless, lame, or just too weird." You might even laugh out loud as you say them because of how contrary they are to your self-concept.

Here's the deal: it doesn't matter if your mind doesn't believe them at first – *they work anyway*. With repetition over time, your subconscious will begin adapting these new beliefs as reality. Whenever you get angry with yourself and say something like, "I'm such an idiot," you lock the notion of being stupid deeper into your subconscious. When you're in a clearer frame of mind, if someone where to ask you, "Do you *really* think you're an idiot?" - you might say no. But it doesn't matter what you consciously believe – these statements shape your self-concept.

Most people spend all of their time expressing negative thoughts about who they are and the reality they live in. They say things like, "This sucks" or "I hate this" or "I deserve this." There's very little effort or energy spent reflecting what they actually DO have going for them. Instead, they're affirming all the things they don't like about their lives, driving these weak beliefs deeper and deeper until they are no longer challenged.

Here's the big question: do you think it's possible to truly feel great about yourself and worthy of attracting high levels of success into your life if the majority of what you tell yourself is negative?

I didn't think so.

Shad Helmstetter, author of *What to Say When You Talk to Yourself,* studied the power of affirmations extensively. He writes, "You will become what you think about most; your success or failure in anything, large or small, will depend on your programming – what you accept from others, and what you say when you talk to yourself. It is no longer a success theory; it is a simple but powerful fact. Neither luck nor desire has the slightest thing to do with it. It makes no difference whether we believe it or not. The brain simply believes what you tell it most. And what you tell it about you, it will create. It has no choice."[20]

What an incredibly simple yet profound concept. If you're still skeptical about how powerful the process of reprogramming your mind is, give it a shot and see how different you feel as a result. You'll discover that utilizing affirmations gives you an excellent tool for mastering your emotional state. Like Helmstetter wrote, what you think about most determines how you feel about yourself.

As you begin saying these out loud repeatedly, keep in mind a few rules to follow:

- Keep them short and to the point

- Keep them positive (don't say "I have NO problems in my life" - declare "my life is relaxed and at ease" instead)

- Put them in the present tense (don't say, "I will..." - say "I am" or "I now have")

- Add emotional energy to them. Saying them mechanically without any enthusiasm won't do much for you.

Here are some examples:

"I act in spite of my fear – I'm a warrior."

"I deserve the highest and very best in life."

"I am worthy and deserving of massive success and abundance."

"I am driven, focused, and know exactly where I'm going in life."

Just like visualization, the more you can get into the emotions of how these affirmations make you feel as you say them, the more powerful they are. If you can get into the habit of doing this every morning at a high energy level for five to ten minutes, you will literally launch into each day feeling amazing and in a peak state. You'll feel like there is NOTHING that can stop you.

In addition to doing these daily, look to do them whenever you need an immediate boost in state. If you are moments away from a major sale, presentation, performance, or sporting event, creating a simple mantra for yourself locks you into a great state and fires you up. Before I do anything really important, I tell myself, "I'm an unstoppable force of nature - let's do this" and I tap my chest repeatedly. Experiment with what feels comfortable to you and know this practice is always available to you whenever needed. Watch what happens to your self-assurance and poise when you realize how quickly you can transition into an empowering frame of mind.

 The Gemstone Principles

Once you're able to generate peak state, you need a few tools you can utilize when you run into stumbling blocks. Clearly, not every day is going to flow the way you want or expect to. You could allow these obstacles to get the best of you, but that wouldn't really speak to the title of this book. You want to know how to keep your cool no matter what gets thrown your way - and these principles address exactly that.

What I'm about to share with you are what I call the Gemstone Principles. Just as gemstones must be discovered, cut, and polished before they become valuable, merely reading this information won't add much to your journey. However, if you make the efforts to not only understand these principles and what they mean to you, but to practice them daily, you will see global changes throughout your life. In fact, it will take a lot for someone to piss you off, intimidate you, or weaken your resolve.

These three principles are some of the biggest discoveries I've either personally found to be true or have gleaned from experts in happiness, peak state, and inner peace. Refer to them after a rough day at work, when you're in an awkward situation, or when you feel otherwise down on your luck. Cut them from this book, polish them by applying the ideas to your life, and discover their enduring power.

The Sapphire Principle

Main Concept:

If we interpret nothing to be an attack on our self-concept, nothing lowers our confidence.

Explanation:

Most of our unhappiness comes as an affront to our self-concept - when we believe that what's happening to us is damaging our self-esteem. If we take an outside event to mean that we're less wise, powerful, loved, or valuable, our state plummets immensely.

Naturally, we feel the most confident when our self-concept is supported or enhanced. Most of the goals that we strive for are tied into our self-esteem; we want to do more and have more so that we can feel better about ourselves. I would argue that the happiest moments in our lives are when we feel that our self-concept is the most appreciated. When our minds recognize evidence for thinking highly of ourselves, we access far more empowered behavior.

However, when our minds locate evidence for the *opposite*, we run into trouble. An insult could be tossed your way, you might do something embarrassing in public, forget about an important assignment, commit a glaring mistake, or otherwise encounter a potentially negative incident. These outside events activate a series of thoughts that determine you should feel less confident about yourself. You then might beat yourself up verbally, attack another person for insulting you, hide from the conversation, or make an excuse to cover up your damaged identity. During these moments, it can be easy to feel like a wounded animal trying to find safety.

However, this perception of inferiority only becomes real for you to the degree that you ACCEPT it. Remember that nothing anyone ever says or does carries any inherent significance until your mind assigns it meaning. Even the most ruthless cheap shot someone attacks you with is hollow and inconsequential until your brain says, "See! I knew it! He's right – you really are a complete loser!" If you can grasp this one simple idea, you will remain in control during tough situations: your confidence will only take a hit when you accept that on some level, what's happening is proof that your self-concept has become damaged.

Imagine you and your wife take your three-year-old son for a trip to the playground. Your wife watches the little guy run around and make new friends while you tell her you'd like to settle down for a nice quick nap underneath a nearby oak tree. You nod off and sleep for a good fifteen minutes until you're suddenly stirred awake with a sharp CLUNK against your head. You jolt up, rub your head in confusion, and scan the playground for the toddler responsible for the mischief. You are getting increasingly agitated as you can't seem to find any clues; no parents are apologizing and no children are even paying you attention. "As soon as I find out who did this, I'm going to give them a piece of my mind," you think to yourself.

But seconds later, you feel another CLUNK. Where is it coming from? You scan the perimeter again with nothing in sight...then...CLUNK there it is again! But this time, you look up and realize a few acorns have been falling out of the tree. With this discovery, every ounce of anger within you disappears immediately. You laugh it off, rejoin your family, and forget about the incident altogether.

So what happened? One second you were furious and looking for someone to blame and the next, you were able to immediately dismiss it. The reason you felt so angry was because you believed someone was attacking your self-concept – and you believed this attack was damaging your identity. When you realized your self-esteem wasn't under assault and that it was OK, you were relaxed again. Same tree, same acorn, two completely different meanings.

By definition, insecurity is the belief that you are under attack or about to be under attack from someone. It's the assumption that the outside world is a THREAT to you. To feel completely secure and at peace, understand that nothing is ever a hazard to your self-concept unless you decide that it is. If you will hold to this realization, you will no longer fear rejection or embarrassment. You will remain confident and at ease as long as you believe your self-concept is secure.

There is a telling scene in the film *Fight Club* that illustrates this point in a unique way. Tyler Durden, played by Brad Pitt, is hosting underground fights in the basement of a bar owned by a large, angry man named Lou. When Lou finds out about this fight club taking place, he confronts Tyler and demands that he shut it down. When Tyler doesn't back down, Lou attacks him in every possible way; he insults him, threatens him, punches him, and essentially beats the living snot out of him. Yet, Tyler reacts by laughing it off and even inviting Lou to join the club – *while* he gets pummeled. This unwavering confidence leads to Tyler grabbing Lou and demanding that he allow the group to continue using the basement. By getting face to face with him and letting his blood pour all over him, Tyler freaks the big guy out and convinces him to support their meetings. What's interesting to note is that Tyler never tries any of the tactics Lou uses; he doesn't throw any punches or insults at him. In fact, he wins the battle between the two by proving how utterly *comfortable* he is with the abuse he's receiving. He shows that not only does his self-concept and identity remain intact throughout all of this, but that his commitment to the group has only gotten stronger.

In Don Miguel Ruiz' book *The Four Agreements*, the author shares four ideas that cultivate a sense of personal freedom. His second agreement is simply "Don't Take Anything Personally." Ruiz

171

argues that nothing other people do is because of you – what they say and do is a projection of their own inner reality and beliefs. If you simply refuse to take anything personally, you won't fall victim to a wounded ego; you will recognize that the attack is really not about you at all. You can reject the notion that your self-concept is being threatened by simply not accepting that what you're seeing or hearing concerns you. At that point, you are free from getting your emotions wrapped up in the negativity of others.[21]

Likewise, Ruiz also suggests that you refrain from taking *compliments* personally as well – to the extent that you don't depend on them to define your self-esteem. Just as insults are merely a projection of a person's weak self-esteem, high praise is usually a projection of a person's strong self-esteem. This isn't to say that you should shun everything positive your friends are trying to express to you – by all means, welcome sincere appreciation. Just don't hang your hat on it and then crave it when you notice you are no longer receiving it.

How to Apply This to Your Life:

If you are ever insulted or threatened, take a deep breath and remind yourself that you don't accept anything being said. Flash a big smile across your face to immediately demonstrate your rejection of these ideas and your amusement of the other person's behavior. Allow the person to vomit everything toxic out of his system, and then show compassion for their anguish. Say something like, "Life must be hard for you today." Do absolutely nothing else to react to this person; walk away from them the way you would walk away from a fart.

If you do something embarrassing, like tripping, spilling a drink, or fumbling a portion of a speech, immediately begin laughing at yourself. During these moments, your conditioned mind wants to belittle you, having you say things like, "I'm such an idiot!" However, your laughter will dissipate this violence it wants to commit against you. By laughing, you fully accept the present moment, and you accept that making mistakes is fine and doesn't affect your self-esteem. Just brush yourself off, maintain loose and relaxed body language, and continue doing whatever you were doing. Any time you feel a surge of negativity returning, just start laughing again.

If you fail or come up short with reaching an important goal, immediately disrupt any frustration you might be feeling toward your self-concept. Do two things as soon as possible: first, make a list of your biggest successes in life – all the areas where you set goals and achieved them. Second, utilize this concept featured in chapter six: treat your world like a personal laboratory. Think about the results you received from your "experiment," what you learned, what you will do differently, and how to apply these ideas to your life. Strip away all negative emotion from your mind the second you realize you're not going to reach a specific goal. Focus instead on what lies ahead – and how you can implement your new lessons into a better strategy.

The Ruby Principle

Main Concept:

The less self-conscious you are and the more you focus on the happiness of others, the more confident you will feel.

Explanation:

In Matthieu Ricard's book, *Happiness: A Guide to Life's Most Important Skill*, he explains that selfishness corrodes our emotional state:

"Selfishness is the source of most of our disruptive thoughts. From obsessive desire to hatred, not to mention jealousy, it attracts pain the way a magnet attracts iron fillings."

We'd all consider someone who is clearly only interested in his own wellbeing an extremely selfish person - I'm sure you've come across plenty of people who were only concerned with fulfilling their own desires. These are the people that attract negative attention their way on a consistent basis; you just want to roll your eyes and ignore these poor souls. However, we rarely consider that a highly self-conscious person is also extremely selfish for similar reasons. These are the people that are only concerned with their personal wellbeing, appearance, happiness, or safety. With all of their thoughts revolving around themselves, they leave no space for the present situation and the people in it. Spotting a self-conscious person is something we all do easily, and these types of people give us little desire to be around them.

Here's a huge point: you feel directly confident to the proportion you believe you are making others feel "good." If you are totally selfless around other people and genuinely focused on raising everyone else's emotional state, your mood rises exponentially. You've already experienced this any time you've told a funny joke or story; someone else's laughter made you feel great because you put them in a better mood.

This principle reflects the Sapphire Principle in that people crave a boost of self-esteem and will do anything possible to avoid a loss of self-esteem. Picture everyone holding an imaginary "tip jar" they keep with them at all times that goes toward how they feel about themselves. You fill the jar by expressing or doing things to make a person feel better about him or herself. You diminish the jar every time you put your needs over theirs, ignore them, judge them, or criticize them. When you make a conscious effort to fill up these tip jars without expecting anyone to fill up yours, you'll find that your self-esteem rises easily.

As long as your efforts to elevate the emotions in others are authentic and unselfish, they will be embraced and reflected back to you. Just don't make the mistake of trying to help everyone else feel good in order to be accepted. Guys make this mistake frequently when meeting a new woman. They try to prove all the ways they're helpful or meaningful to society by showing off their job and status as a way of saying, "Look at me – I've done this, this, and this for the world." Even worse, they fish out generic compliments for her that don't come across as authentic. These are usually extremely self-centered because they communicate, "I like you – I really like you. You should like me too...so please like me! Please accept me! I need you to accept me!"

There is a difference between PAYING someone a compliment and GIVING someone a compliment. If you PAY someone a compliment, you're expecting something in return. However, if you

GIVE someone a compliment, you're sharing praise without requiring anything back. The difference between the two is the EMOTIONAL WEIGHT that comes with it. The more self-centered your motivation, the more you put weight and pressure on others so that you can stand taller. The less self-centered you are, the more you lift others up, automatically raising your spirits. Which person would you rather hang out with?

How to Apply This to Your Life:

I know what you're thinking: "Okay, so the key is to be less self-conscious, but how the hell do I have any control over that?"

Think of it as a muscle you're going to have to exercise in order to get stronger. If you're a highly self-conscious person, it's going to take some work to break the mental habits you've created. The first step is going to be with awareness – recognize when you're the most nervous and worried about what other people are thinking of you. During these moments, just tell yourself, "Okay, I'm focused entirely on myself right now – I need to shift my perspective." Then ask yourself a question about your environment that guides your mind off of you.

Let's say you find yourself in a conversation with a group of people who you believe are more successful than you. You catch your mind starting to drift inwards, worrying if what you're saying is "good enough" for them. As soon as you recognize that you're out of balance, you begin thinking of questions about your environment. You tune in closely to the conversation and hear the woman sitting next to you talking about her new Border Terrier with excitement. You then ask yourself, "Why is she talking about the dog – what kind of emotion does she want us to share with her?" You could then take a page from the Social Gameplan chapter and ask her what her biggest challenges have been with it and what her favorite aspect of owning it is.

More important than what you say to her is showing her that you're totally present to what she's saying. I've noticed that if I'm ever a part of a group discussion and I don't know much about what's being said or otherwise feel out of place, if I simply give receptive body language by nodding my head, making strong eye contact, and smiling, I connect with the group. Rather than disengage mentally from the conversation, I find that I tend to invest more of myself to it. I ask more questions, make more observations, and give more energy to connect with the people there.

The situations where you find yourself comfortable and naturally un-self-conscious are going to be easy to you; they won't take much mental discipline to maintain a healthy balance of self-awareness. However, the circumstances that bring more inner scrutiny are going to demand more effort from you – you can't check out and hide in your own thoughts. Often we mistakenly believe a group is ignoring us or giving us negative attention when we become self-conscious. Something like, "I guess I'm not really wanted here" can easily cross our minds. In reality, the group is just not seeing much involvement from us. By simply increasing your attention and empathy, you allow people to engage more with you. If they're a high quality group, they will always work to meet you halfway.

As a whole, you can always apply this principle in small doses by giving sincere compliments as often as you can. Just get into the habit of challenging yourself to share one aspect of genuine appreciation in some way whenever you spend time with your friends and family. Even a few kind words here or there will make a tremendous difference in a person's life. Think about the last time someone gave you authentic praise for who you are and how it made you feel. Look to return the favor as often as humanly possible.

Another great habit to get into is to share as much value with the world as you can for free without expecting any return on your time or energy. Teach someone a skill or technique you're gifted in, help someone out with a project, volunteer to do a favor for a friend, or coach a buddy through a tough decision. On a larger scale, you can always volunteer for a cause, mentor a student, or raise money to help the world. If you simply make it a priority to GIVE more value to the community than you TAKE from it, you will be rewarded hundreds of times over.

Always keep a finger on the pulse of how the people around you are feeling. If you're out socially with friends and see someone out of place, pull them into the conversation. Give them a high five,

176

take a picture with them, ask if they want another drink, or introduce them to someone they haven't met yet. If you just assume that your self-concept is strong and that you're an awesome guy with no need to prove anything to anyone, you free up all of your inner resources to lifting up those around you. If that doesn't make you a great guy, I have no idea what does.

The Emerald Principle

Main Concept:

Allow life to come to you instead of struggling towards it. The more you struggle to get the results you want, the more you push them away. Be effortless, relaxed, and detached from your desired outcome to attract it to you instead.

Explanation:

When we have a specific result we would like to achieve, our minds tend to demand a lot of mental energy from us. We formulate strategies, conceive new angles, and usually give all of our effort into what we want. After trying the strategy for a while, if we don't see the results we're looking for, we work even harder. Before we think of new concepts, we try the same strategies with more effort and struggle even more for what we want. The problem is that our behavior shows up as forced and pressured, and this pressure actually pushes away what we desire.

Think of the last time you visited a friend's house for the first time and got a chance to meet their cat. To those who are inexperienced with cats, the strategy is often to approach the animal the same way one would a dog: walking right up, giving it plenty of attention, and basically just grabbing it. But for those who know a bit more about the pet, this never works. The trick is to simply behave as if one is detached completely from the situation - almost as if they don't even care. Then, often when a person is completely relaxed, the cat will come and introduce itself. Try for yourself and see how easy it is get a cat's attention by letting it come to you instead of going after it.

As men, we usually apply the masculine approach of completing our goals to each and every circumstance. Our strategy is to use our minds to figure out a course of action, and then stick to it until we get what we want. If we have to struggle along the way and smash our head against a few walls, so be it – we stand by the 'no pain, no gain' motto with pride. We will smash the square peg into the round hole until it has no choice but to cooperate.

While there is nothing inherently wrong or incorrect with this mode of operation, I suggest balancing in the feminine approach to life as well. You do this by allowing life to come to you and ATTRACTING what you want to fall into place. While having a warrior psyche is necessary to persevere when life tosses obstacles in your path and demands you to overcome them, sometimes you need a different mindset to find success.

Here's what the process looks like: formulate a clear and specific strategy, take concentrated action, and then relax and detach your emotions from the desired result. Recall the concept of emotional weight from chapter three: don't emotionally "lean" onto what you want. Don't struggle to make the universe bend to your wishes; if something isn't working, try a different approach altogether. Trust that what you're looking for is going to meet you halfway and simply relax.

In Mihaly Csikszentmihaly's book *Flow*, the author takes a look at the state of mind people take on when experiencing "flow" - the inner feeling of joy and contentment where one doesn't think about his or her problems and simply focuses entirely on the present moment. This happens when your brain isn't working to control a situation and is allowed to simply relax into it. There's no pressure on your mind to actively "figure it all out" - it has the freedom to develop great ideas as they arise from the subconscious.[22]

Practice flow by enjoying the process and coming to terms with the fact that you will often not know what's going to happen next at any given moment. Instead of surrendering to the temptation of needing to figure out what's going to happen before it occurs, trust that you will be prepared to handle anything that comes your way. Accept that something new and different is always around the corner, and rely on your subconscious mind to know exactly what to do with it. Let the present moment flow into the future without any restriction.

How to Apply This to Your Life:

When you find yourself in a situation where you want to be witty, spontaneous, or coming up with funny things off the top of your head, don't try to be any of these things. Completely eliminate the pressure and instead allow your witty knowledge to simply come to you. Think of the perfect joke or killer one-liner as the cat you want to attract into your orbit. Don't force your mind to capture it - let it find you instead.

Trust that all of your clever jokes, funny stories, amazing ideas, and brilliant thoughts are instantly available to you on tap. The only thing you need to do is get the engine started by listening to the thousands of incredible thoughts already inside you and express them as they arise. The more you become accustomed to trusting your mental faculties, the more you will attract creative thoughts your way. If you still find that your mind is drawing a total blank, don't let yourself get frustrated; remember to stay detached emotionally. Just say, "Well I thought I had something amazing here swirling around in my memory – guess you'll have to wait until next time to hear it." Ironically, this nonchalance is exactly what gives you more confidence in freely expressing yourself.

If you're answering questions during a high-pressure job interview, instead of trying to formulate perfect responses, allow your mind to bring you the answers you need in a relaxed manner. Breathe in deeply, pause, and imagine your mind serving you what needs to be said on a platter. The more you force the responses you think are best, the harder it will be to say them, and the more robotic you'll come across. Believe that everything you're saying is gold, and that you don't need it all to completely land. Heck, you don't even need the job; you're a total badass, remember?

When you meet a beautiful girl for the first time, let everything your mind gives you flow without hesitation. Again, trust that all of

179

the clever thoughts you're looking for are coming to you, and all you have to do is relax and focus your attention on the moment. If your mind is ever blank, simply smile, take a big breath, and lay back. Show her that you're comfortable with silence.

Speaking of women, they love MYSTERY. Rather than operating with the metaphor of *chasing* after your next date, think of *attracting* her into your life. You do this by inviting her slowly into your world, not revealing every piece of information about yourself up front, and even withholding key aspects of your life journey to arouse curiosity. Rather than behaving like most men who seem to strong arm their greatness into the minds of their dates, leave it up to her to discover your greatness for herself. This process of having to work to get to know you is far more magnetic to her than giving her all the keys right away.

Remember, be the WANTED man, not the WANTING man.

 Elevate Your Energy

Let me share with you a simple formula for attraction:

HIGH ENERGY = HIGH ATTRACTION

Your energy is a direct reflection of your personal power. The more you experience high energy, the more you elevate the emotions of those around you. You can tell when you meet someone with strong energy; everything they communicate has resonance and power. You feel their vitality and strength by just being close to them. They are difficult to forget because of how intense their presence is; the ideas they express have a lot of momentum behind them. In fact, the most charismatic people you have ever met likely have had more energy than those you normally speak to. Your emotional state is affected on a higher level by being around them.

Most of the world tends to operate at a lower, more lethargic energy level. This probably evolved from the evolutionary advantage of conserving stamina when possible. By avoiding unnecessary effort, our ancestors lowered their need for food and were able to keep enough in the tank to escape predators when needed. However in today's world, the key to making a lasting impact is to be generous with your output of energy. To be a more attractive person, you simply need to share more vitality with people when you speak with them. Rather than conserving your spirit in an effort to appear cool or low-key, give it away often and freely.

You'll find that by expending more energy, not only do you become a more magnetic person, but you also enjoy what you're doing more. University of Southern California Neuroscientist Antonio Damasio describes his three keys to "maximal harmonious states" as:

1. Full Attention

2. Enthusiastic Interest

3. Positive Emotional Intensity[23]

These three things require more energetic output than a person typically gives during the day. Think about the last time you gave something your FULL attention – no distractions, no mental chatter – just being totally consumed with focus. Now consider the last time you showcased a high amount of enthusiasm for something. The billion-dollar question then is: when was the last time you felt BOTH simultaneously?

The key to getting more out of life is to simply invest more energy into all that you do. If you want to receive more recognition, attention, and appreciation from the world, give more of your vitality to it. Give more attention and concentration to the people you're speaking to, demonstrate enthusiasm for who they are and what they speak about, and practice the gemstone principles for maintaining a strong emotional state. In order to receive more, simply BE more – elevate your energy on an ongoing basis.

Charging the Battery

In order to deliver a strong amount of energy, you need to effectively charge your battery. You accomplish this by giving your body what it needs so that your reserves are available when necessary. You won't be able to affect change or influence when you're running on E – so make sure you take the extra time to incorporate these strategies into your daily schedule.

Let's start with the obvious: make sure you are getting plenty of sleep at night. You need at least seven hours to function at your best. Also, if you find that you're still crashing around mid-day, allow yourself a twenty-minute nap. A NASA study led by David Dinges found that short naps lead to an increase in performance and alertness later in the day. This is probably why many European countries accommodate time for naps during the workday.

In addition to sleeping more often, be sure you are getting plenty of sunlight. Your body has its own unique temperature that rises and falls at set times during the day. The cooler your body temperature, the more tired you feel. To feel more awake, simply expose your eyes to more sunlight. This warms your body's internal temperature and leads to you feeling more energized. (Just don't be stupid and stare directly into the sun). The vitamin D also helps sustain your body in ways that your diet alone isn't providing. It's no coincidence that most people complain about being tired all of the time and yet spend 99% of their time indoors – driving to work, sitting in a cubicle, driving back home, and vegetating in front of the TV.

Another obvious yet often neglected area is making sure you drink plenty of water. If you roughly divide your body weight in half, you will have the number of ounces you need to drink daily. Your body is basically 60% water – you need it to flush out toxins and waste products in your system. Without consistent hydration, you are going to start winding down by mid-afternoon. Keep a water bottle with you throughout the day, or at the very least, make an effort to drink a full glass of water every few hours. Even mild dehydration can contribute to feeling tired.

Lastly, if you can get into the habit of exercising in the morning instead of at night, you will have a stronger mood and energy level. Your body temperature will begin rising during your workout and you will feel more alert and prepared to handle the day's tasks. This has a domino effect throughout the day; you begin the morning with high energy, which spills over into your afternoon, which then powers you through your evening. If you're a night owl and find yourself working out in the evening and wonder why it's difficult for you to sleep at night, this is an area you need to examine. When you exercise at night, you stimulate your metabolism, raise your body's temperature, and encourage your nervous system to keep you active for the next few hours. To help you get plenty of sleep, I recommend working out no later than six PM.

In spite of utilizing these tips, you might have an unrelenting schedule that demands you to work through fatigue anyways. We've all had moments when we're totally wiped out and yet have hours of work ahead of us. For this reason, I've concocted my own technique for recharging my battery whenever I feel exhausted. I call it the Five Minute Lightning Round.

The first thing I do is grab my iPod, throw on a song with a fast tempo, and crank up the volume. I will then stand up, take a few deep breaths in and out, and close my eyes. I'll let the music guide my body according to the rhythm, and I'll begin bouncing around, gradually picking up my pace as the song picks up. If I'm particularly drained, I'll actually take some more deep breaths and then yell a little bit when I exhale. This shifts my emotional state quickly, which helps my entire body wake up. About halfway through the song, I'll start reciting my favorite affirmation while I tap my chest: "All right, you got this – you're an unstoppable force of nature. Let's do this. Wake up! Let's go!" As I'm saying these declarations, I'm increasing the tempo, saying them faster each time. Generally within this five-minute window, I have enough of a charge going to power through another hour or two of the day.

Leveraging music this way to affect your emotional state is extremely powerful. As you dance and move your body with it, blood and oxygen circulate faster and easier. This breaks up the blocks of fatigue and frees you up to reclaim some much-needed energy. I encourage you to utilize the Five Minute Lightning Round whenever you feel too tired to press on.

Be the Life of the Party

People tend to gravitate toward high energy individuals like moths to a flame. When a person is engaging several people at once and moving around a group, the eyes in the room will drift toward him. Our eyes are also trained to pay attention to movement and to essentially ignore things that remain still. This is why it's important to be expending your energy when you're at social gatherings; you won't catch much positive attention sitting on a couch.

I know what some of you are thinking: "Coach, what if I'm naturally a low-key guy?" That's cool, and if you apply everything I've taught you so far, you will be just fine. But you'll never take your influence to the next level because excellence requires more energy. If suddenly becoming a more spirited person is too big of a leap for you, then build it up in small increments. Infuse more passion into the stories you tell. Laugh louder and harder. Use more gestures and take up space when you talk. Do one extra thing you wouldn't normally do to express yourself.

Earlier in this chapter we discussed the importance of taking responsibility for your emotional state. You always have control over how you feel in any given circumstances, and if you do your best to start each day by launching into a strong state, practicing the Three Gemstone Principles to maintain it, and taking care of your body to elevate your energy, you're going to consistently feel awesome.

Now let's take your education to the level of mastery. Once you acquire the ability to control your emotions and can rely on yourself to be in a great mood at any given moment, take on a greater responsibility. *Consider it your duty now to become the life of the party everywhere you go.*

Recall the Ruby Principle: the more you focus on the happiness of others, the more confident you will feel. This is half of what being the party is all about – your concentration needs to lie outside of you. The other half concerns your energy; it will take active engagement and effort to truly pull this off. You won't be able to do this by sitting quietly alone while feeling amazing – yes you will feel at peace with everything, but you won't impact anyone's life.

Here's a powerful affirmation to try on for size: "I am the party that others are looking for." Recite this aloud a few times moments before attending any kind of party, networking event, club, bar, or social scene. Before you spend time with new acquaintances, hype yourself up this way to launch into a strong emotional state and set your intention for your time in the space.

As soon as you enter the social gathering, start to actively work the room. Make it a priority to meet as many guests as possible, utilizing the networking skills you picked up in chapter six to create engaging conversations. Rather than standing off to the side and hoping to catch a few people walking by, be proactive with your time. A good rule of thumb is to assume that no one is going to approach you within the first half hour – you need to generate the connections.

Plan on spending just enough time with each person to create a bond by showing genuine interest in who they are but do not waste time with negative people. As soon as you sense a weird vibe going on, quickly change the subject and walk away. You need to guard your own emotional state the way you would a precious diamond; you'll find it thousands of times more difficult to uplift the spirit of the party with yours being dragged down.

Once you've created several connections with the guests, look to introduce one another where appropriate. For example, if you meet a recent college graduate who is desperately looking for a job in administrative work and a friendly HR Executive who could probably help, grab the college grad and drag her over to introduce them. This process of constantly weaving people together is called forming "triads" by entrepreneur and best-selling author Eben Pagan. He argues that if you're routinely doing this, you're not only boosting the energy in the room throughout the party, you're actually keeping it going.

At this point, you can expect people to begin approaching you out of curiosity. By seeing you perpetually in motion, bringing a variety of personalities together, and raising the room's energy, you position yourself as the social leader. Within an hour or less, your presence can change an entire event completely.

I challenge you to apply this to your social game plan according to your personality. If you have a great sense of humor, bring the party by sharing your jokes with more people. If you are an excellent conversationalist, bring the party by connecting more deeply with each new person. If you're gifted at dancing, singing, acting, or public speaking, show off your skills more often. Be the party that others are looking for.

8

UNWAVERING PRESENCE

"The man who does not concentrate will be either a half success, a mediocrity, or a complete failure." – Orison Swett Marden

If chapter seven was all about training your emotions, this chapter is all about training your *mind*. You can think of this section as mental training because in order to master confidence, you must develop a strong mindset that doesn't sabotage you with negative thoughts and distractions. So you're going to learn how to give your mind a workout in order to strengthen your control over it. You'll discover that disciplining your thoughts this way allows you to gain clarity on what distracts you and weakens your power the most.

When you have unwavering presence, every cell in your body is directed toward the same mission, rather than scattering off in several directions. This unison of focus allows the energy behind your expressions to land with far more impact; you communicate in shock waves instead of weak ripples. You have the ability to

187

truly influence others' lives because most of us aren't accustomed to absorbing this much concentrated energy.

If you study the most charismatic and influential leaders in history, they all share this huge thing in common: a laser-like focus on one clear mission they refuse to stray from. They became so single-minded in their communication that no one could distract, persuade, or knock them off course. One would almost get the sense that the mission was ALL the leader was ever thinking about. This mental discipline is precisely why they gave some of the most influential speeches of all time; every single word was delivered with power.

I'm not sure exactly what kind of person you are. You might be inspired to create a mission you wish to share with the world in order to change some lives. You may simply want to just develop more charisma when speaking with others. Regardless of your ambitions, downloading these ideas into your brain will generate immediate improvements in your ability to hold another person's attention. Fittingly, your capacity to hold attention *yourself* is the key to obtaining this.

In this chapter you'll learn:

- How to stay centered or present even during difficult situations

- How to direct your thoughts through concentration to increase your power

- How to apply meditation to your life and instantly increase your peace of mind

- How to practice discipline and self-control

- How to rise above the limitations of your ego and discover true confidence

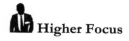 **Higher Focus**

When I talk about focus, I'm talking about two different things: concentration and awareness. Concentration is your central vision – narrow, zoomed in, and fixed on one specific thing at a time. Awareness is your peripheral vision – zoomed out, wide, and prepared to handle or ignore potential distractions. Both elements are crucial to master your thoughts and to get a complete grip on your surroundings.

These two skills can and must be strengthened over time to reach a high level of confidence. Ideally you are mentally built like an oak tree – its branches may bend and break with strong gusts of wind, its leaves may shake with the breeze, but its body doesn't flinch even in the face of tornadoes, hurricanes, and storms thanks to its roots' grip in the soil. This piece of the book is all about strengthening these roots so that it will take an eighteen-wheeler to knock you over.

Concentration Cultivation

Most of us are terrible at focusing on one thing at a time for longer than a handful of minutes. We browse the internet, text our buddies, answer or make phone calls, check our email, and talk to our friends close by when working on major projects. When it's time to leave work for the day and enjoy some free time with our family, we fail to get all of our work done, so we play catch up while only being semi-available to our loved ones. Instead of concentrating 100% of our attention towards one thing at a time, we end up splitting it in several directions at once. We give about 50% of our minds to our work while we're there, and then get home and give about 50% to our family while we're with them.

We let ourselves get distracted so easily and often succumb to multi-tasking by doing three or four things at the same time. Have you ever tried to simply sit still for ten minutes in quiet relaxation with your eyes closed? No cell phone, no internet, no working, no planning...just relaxing? For most of us, even the simple act of doing this is impossible.

In Alain De Botton's 2010 essay on Distraction, he makes this keen observation: "To sit still and think without succumbing to an anxious reach for a machine has become almost impossible."[24] While the human race has made thousands of incredible advancements that have helped in productivity and made our lives easier, we now have access to thousands of potential disruptions to our concentration. With more breakthroughs coming every year, I'd be willing to bet that we're only going to see more get in our way.

If you were to take a closer look into the brain of the average person, you would see a million thoughts trying to fire simultaneously. Our thought patterns usually look like, "Okay I only have another hour to get this done – I really need to get to work here...oh look a new email...did I take out the trash?...what am I going to eat for lunch?...there's no way I'm going to get this done in time...I can't believe she blew me off for lunch...wow I'm tired...I can't think of anything...what am I supposed to be doing?" Our minds get so tangled up in all these ideas flying around that it's seemingly impossible to select one to pay attention to at a time. To make matters worse, our environments are getting louder with so many messages competing for your attention as well. Have you noticed that advertisements seem to be popping up *everywhere* now? It's no wonder we're such poor listeners.

Mihaly Csikszentmihalyi states this in his book *Flow*: "The individual mind can only process so much at a time. It has to be selective to function. The info we allow into consciousness becomes extremely important; it is in fact what determines the content and quality of life."[25]

To improve your concentration, you need to understand that the most important aspect isn't what you're paying attention to. It's really about what you're NOT paying attention to. It's actively CHOOSING where your mind is going to expend its energy instead of letting it run in fifteen different directions. Research has repeatedly proven that we're far more productive and efficient when we choose to do one thing at a time rather than multitask. This discipline comes in the ability to block out what's not important so we can selectively focus on the one thing that will benefit us the most in the present moment. This is critical to accomplishing more, feeling happier, and overcoming difficult obstacles.

The first changes you must begin making concern ignoring unwanted distractions and keeping them off your radar. At any given moment, ask yourself, "What is the single most important thing I could be concentrating on right now?" Once you decide, eliminate every single potential diversion you can. If you're wrapping up a research paper in college, shut off your computer's internet connection while you work, put your cell phone on silent, and head somewhere you won't be bothered. If you're having an important conversation with a loved one, move somewhere quiet if your environment is too busy or make sure the eye contact for both of you remains constant. If you're performing on stage or during a sporting event, leave your worries at the door so that you can give your complete attention to your execution.

A lot of improving your concentration just boils down to being mindful about these distractions. If you've gotten into the habit of multitasking or letting your brain run in several directions at once, it may be challenging to notice what's disrupting your concentration because thinking about multiple things at once is normal for you. I want to make it clear that being totally and completely focused on only one thing at a time throughout our entire life is really not possible. However, waking up to the things that distract you the most gives you some much needed clarity.

At some point today, sit in complete silence for five minutes. Your purpose during this time is not to completely quiet the mind, but rather to pay attention to what kind of thoughts seem to want to distract you the most. Observe if you get bored immediately – find out what your mind would rather you do instead. See what kinds of problems or worries break into your thoughts that demand solutions. Notice all of the irrelevant chatter your brain shares with you. Then write down the three biggest thoughts that come up. These are the three distractions you're going to want to work to eliminate first.

You can weaken these distractions' power over you by noticing them as soon as they show up. When you do, ignore them to the best of your ability. Feel the temptation to stray off course and give your attention to them, and right before you do, catch yourself in the act to stop the habit. Let's say your biggest distraction is watching Youtube videos while you know you should be devoting your attention to work. As soon as you feel the urge to open up your browser and watch a video of a cat smacking a toddler in the face, catch yourself in the act by recognizing the impulse. If it helps, silently say something like, "Not now – gotta stay focused." Then take a deep breath and resume the work. The more you do this, the more your brain becomes wired to stay on track.

I want to make an obvious point here: I'm not suggesting that you become a workaholic and avoid entertaining distractions entirely. Heaven knows I'm as big a fan of that cat smacking toddler video as anyone out there. I'm encouraging you to simply do one thing at a time – only work when you've set aside time to work and only play when you've set aside time to play.

The next time you have a conversation with someone one on one who you feel isn't very confident, pay attention to their ability to concentrate. Just listen to what they're saying and how they're saying it. You'll find that their ideas don't flow together and don't really lead anywhere, their eyes dart around the environment and their attention fades in and out of your time together, and they fidget constantly with their body language out of boredom and absent-mindedness.

Conversely, when you speak to someone you feel is powerful and influential, notice how laser-focused they are with their attention. Their sentences are crisp and to the point. They maintain great eye contact with you both while they speak and while you speak. They seem to be giving you 100% of their focus during the entire conversation. Their body language is purposeful and direct; they don't expend nervous energy in unnecessary gestures. The more you sharpen your own ability to concentrate, the more you will recognize how well or how poorly others can focus as well.

Another strategy for improving your concentration involves putting yourself directly into environments with plenty of potential distractions. For example, the next time you visit a crowded and noisy restaurant with a good friend, keep your thoughts centered on your table's conversation only. As other tables next to you start laughing, yelling, and offering noisy distractions, keep your eyes locked on your friend. Don't allow them to wander over somewhere else at any time – no matter how badly you want to check out what's happening. This practice will help you stay focused when you need to the most – you'll be better equipped to keep your composure with a lot coming at you simultaneously.

Expanding Awareness

While concentration is all about focusing on just one thing at a time, awareness is your ability to sense the entirety of what's going on around you. This is your peripheral vision – driving forty miles an hour and seeing a child on a bicycle heading into the road out of the corner of your eye and slamming on the brakes. Your understanding of your surroundings and what's taking place in your environment is key.

When you're oblivious to your surroundings, you can be startled and lose composure easily. You will produce more knee-jerk reactions from getting thrown out of balance unexpectedly. However, if you have a finger on the pulse of life around you, you'll be ready to handle the unforeseen surprises. If something crashes into your reality, you will be calmly prepared to handle it without freaking out. When you have the mental strength to control your responses and do what's necessary quickly, you have high awareness.

Recall how the mind's RAS system works. We tend to react to what's LOUD and potentially HARMFUL to our safety. If you don't sharpen your mental awareness, your mind can easily convince you that too many things demand your attention and are potential threats to you. Losing control over your thoughts in this manner can often lead to you losing control over your environment. For example, if you're in a noisy bar and accidentally bump into a hulking two hundred and eighty pound linebacker, if he steps up to you and starts yelling in your face, will you completely let go of the reins or will you maintain focus? Will you have the ability to calmly diffuse the situation or will you panic and let it escalate?

This boils down to two concepts: your ability to respond in a quick and automatic fashion (your reaction time) and your ability to refrain from reacting altogether when necessary. With any circumstance that tests your awareness, one of these abilities will show up and influence the outcome. Let's say that you do indeed have a humongous linebacker screaming in your face. One alternative would be to respond by *not* reacting. Simply take deep breaths, maintain your stance without backing down, allow him to yell at you as much as he feels he needs to, take complete accountability for bumping into him, and then calmly offer an apology. If he's not backing down and seems keen on starting a fight with you, your other option is to respond quickly by assessing your environment. Locate the nearest bouncer and start inching toward him, find your friends and signal them over to you, and find the nearest exit (which is probably going to be toward the back of the establishment). How quickly you discover these three things and take conscious action towards them will dictate how successful you are in avoiding the fight. Of course, if you're trained in martial arts and prepared to fight, your reaction time will be immediately tested as you would likely resort to blocking an attack in self-defense.

With that being said, let's take a closer look at the first half of high awareness (reaction time) and what you can do to improve it. One of the most efficient ways for boosting this skill is by improving your peripheral vision. Having strong peripheral vision will help you locate movement outside of your central vision easier, allowing you to dodge incoming objects, notice changes in your environment, and be otherwise ready for potential surprises.

A simple way to enhance this is by taking time to focus on the details of objects that lie outside of your central vision. For example, from where you are sitting right now, get a sense of what lies in the outside edges of your eyesight. Try looking straight in front of you while picking two objects, one on each side of you, and paying close attention to their color, shape, and distance from you. Practice doing this simple routine for just a few minutes a day for a week: each time you visit somewhere new and sit down, pick out two new things in your environment and distinguish as many details as possible about them without directly looking at them.

Once you've developed that skill, try incorporating movement. While looking directly in front of you again, have a friend bring different objects in and out of your peripheral vision while you try to guess what they are. With enough repetition, you should be able to accurately identify what they are even if they're being held on the outskirts of what you can actually see.

Once you've mastered your peripheral vision, you can directly increase your reaction time by doing simple exercises that test your speed. Sit with your arm lying across a flat service and extend your hand beyond the edge. Have a friend hold a meter stick (50 cm) vertically above your hand with the "0" end just above your thumb and forefinger. Without warning you, have your partner drop the stick and catch it with your thumb and forefinger as quickly as you can. Record how far the stick fell before you caught it and check out a timetable to figure out your reaction time (Google "meter stick reaction time" to find one). You'll more than likely struggle initially to score higher than .2 seconds, but with practice, you'll increase your speed dramatically.

You can also do the same exercise with a twenty-dollar bill. If the meter stick feels too much like science class all over again (trust me, I hated science) you can make a simple wager: you and your partner alternate turns and whoever catches the money first keeps it. Again, catching the twenty will be tough and seemingly impossible at first, but over time you'll be able to snag it consistently.

Boosting your reaction speed will benefit you in a variety of ways; if you play sports, you're going to have an edge over other athletes. If you're driving and have to swerve the car to avoid an accident, you'll keep everyone with you safe. If you find yourself in an unexpected fight with someone, you'll have a greater chance at successfully defending yourself. In essence, you'll become more instinctive about your environment and prepared to handle threatening situations.

As stated before, the other half of high awareness involves your ability to avoid reaction altogether. If these two ideas sound paradoxical, it's because they are. Sometimes you're going to need to act quickly and decisively while others will require you to simply stand your ground. During these moments, you'll have to prevent an automatic response from triggering inside you that makes you flinch or move without your control.

If you think back to the chapter six section on Intimidation Protocol, you'll realize I suggest ignoring as much of what someone trying to provoke you says as possible. You will find that he is strictly looking for a reaction from you, and that by reacting, you validate his influence over you. The reason that you want to avoid reaction in these scenarios is because it trains your mind to be PROACTIVE and focus only on what you want. If you're constantly responding to stimuli that you don't enjoy or that doesn't serve you, you're burning through precious energy and willpower, which lowers your emotional state *dramatically*.

You'll find that training your mind to shut out distracting and negative stimuli automatically gives you a higher sense of awareness in your environment. This occurs because you free up mental resources to pay more attention to what's actually important to you. If you're incapable of being startled, nothing in your vicinity can make you slip or lose focus. Your attention can hone in on the conversations you're having, the people you're speaking to, and the fun you're creating.

Practice non-reaction on a daily basis. If you're running errands and someone interrupts your train of thought by asking an unexpected question, take a deep breath, relax, and consciously choose what to respond with. Don't just blurt out an automatic response. Try to scare your friends by catching them off guard and have them attempt to scare you. Train yourself to flinch as little as possible, even if you are completely startled. Practice keeping your cool when you hear loud noises and come across unexpected events. Roll with them the same way you would improvise a presentation you lost your notes for.

Applying these strategies toward improving your concentration and awareness will lead to marked changes in your life. However, there is one specific method you can utilize that will boost both of these skills tremendously. If you want to gain mastery over your mind, the answer is through practicing meditation.

 **Meditation**

Meditation is the act of quiet contemplation in order to train and regulate the mind. While there are thousands of different styles and techniques, the only thing required is a steady concentration. You don't need to learn some elaborate chant, contort your legs like a pretzel, or drop everything you're doing for a spiritual retreat to Tibet. By simply closing your eyes and focusing on your breath, you're meditating.

This process is extremely beneficial to raising your ability to focus for a number of reasons. For one, it directly addresses the prefrontal cortex – the part of your brain responsible for attention and concentration. This happens because while a person is meditating, they are actively exercising this area and strengthening it over time. Meditation also physically affects our gray matter, which is involved with sensory perceptions such as hearing, emotions, and speech. To show you how important this stuff is, roughly 95% of all the oxygen you inhale that's set aside for your brain goes directly to it. The more often you meditate, the denser the gray matter becomes - just like a muscle that gets bigger with frequent trips to the gym. You're literally beefing up your brain every time you sit down and do this.

As stated before, there are several different ways to meditate. Ultimately, you're going to want to find a style (or combination of styles) that best suits you. There are three simple methods I'll briefly break down and leave for you to try out.

- Altruistic Compassion – Contemplate a deep sense of compassion for others and the world. Think about everything you love and enjoy about life and imagine people around the globe experiencing the same feelings. Rather than seeing yourself as separate or disconnected from everyone else, see the connection between you and others. Extend as much gratitude as you can for everyone in your life who has helped you in your journey and for everyone you are about to meet. Sustain this emotion for as long as you can during the meditation, and when you notice your thoughts drifting, bring your attention back to it.

- Focused Concentration – Choose one object or aspect of life and focus all of your attention on it. Anything found in nature works well – trees, ocean waves, a candle flame, etc. Anytime a distracting thought rushes into your consciousness, snap your focus back onto the object. Do this over and over again as your mind wants to wander off by thinking about your worries, needs, and desires. If you don't fancy the outdoors, concentrating on your own breath is a perfectly adequate solution. Give all of your attention to the inhale and exhale of air to your lungs. Breathe deeply and direct your concentration back to it when your mind wanders off course.

- Open Awareness – Relax your mind into a state of complete awareness without actively focusing on anything in particular. As new emotions and thoughts come up, don't try to shift your attention. Simply notice and observe them without judgment. While concentration keeps your focus strictly on one object, open awareness allows an unlimited number of things to shift in and out of consciousness. Imagine simply taking a big step outside of your body and just watching your mind and all of the noise it generates. This style of meditation greatly enhances your self-awareness by helping you distinguish how your thoughts impact you and how you then impact your environment.

I suggest that you experiment with these three techniques and discover which work the most for you. Take five to fifteen minutes right when you wake up at the beginning of your day and right before you fall asleep to simply sit in peace. Keeping your back straight, focus on breathing from your diaphragm, and as thoughts come to you, allow them to flow in and out of your consciousness. If you start worrying or thinking about what you need to take care of, simply return to your meditation in a relaxed fashion. Don't worry if you feel like you're "not doing it properly." Any effort you give in quiet contemplation, no matter how much inner chatter you feel distracts you, is beneficial.

You may experience a range of emotions while doing this - gratitude, joy, sadness, anger, guilt, peace, boredom, or excitement can all show up. Be completely open to however you feel during this time without resisting it. Your body and mind are simply releasing stored energy and letting it free.

If you are disciplined enough to do this daily, your overall wellbeing and ability to handle stress will dramatically increase. You'll notice you feel lighter and more carefree during the day and that you won't be as weighed down by fear or nervousness. People will be more attracted to you because of your relaxed energy. As an added benefit, your physical energy will increase and you'll become more capable of mustering up the willpower to do things when you don't want to.

If you could only last a few minutes in total concentration before needing a break prior to meditation, you'll easily double your duration and level of focus. This process just makes you sharper and more in tune with your surroundings. You'll come up with wittier, funnier, and craftier ideas on demand. Without having to press too much, you'll trust your mind to deliver awesome thoughts to you and you'll be quick to express them.

To really gain a huge edge over your competitors – whether it be sports opponents, people applying for the same job as you, guys trying to lure a cute girl you're talking to away from you, or anyone else you go up against – make meditation a priority in your life. You will easily become more noticeably powerful than those who don't meditate on a regular basis. Just like a muscular bodybuilder standing next to a scrawny couch potato, the difference between you will be obvious. As an added bonus, few people will be able to explain why you stand out so much, which adds to your mystery; an invisible force within is generating your power.

 Unwavering Presence

Being present means directing your consciousness to the current moment alone, not thinking about the future or reminiscing about the past. It's being alive in the here and now so that you're giving 100% to what's taking place during the present moment. This boils down to not entertaining every one of the thousand thoughts that pour out of your brain on a daily ongoing basis so you focus only on where you are for one moment in time. This is the crux of the chapter and largely affects your ability to project core confidence.

Humans on average have a new thought show up every eleven seconds. Most of these thoughts tend to be negative or based in fear; they either concern what's going to happen in the future and how you're going to handle it or what happened in the past and what that means to you. Consider how often you imagine scenarios playing out in ways you don't want them to and how often you beat yourself up for mistakes you made in your life. How much time are you wasting worrying or stressing out about these things?

Sometimes we just need to take a break from all of this mental chatter. So take a deep breath right now. Focus your attention completely on the present moment. Feel the slight tingle of energy in your hands and feet. Observe the rise and fall of your chest as you breathe in and out. Plant your feet into the ground and move your toes slowly. Listen to the noises from the world around you – the hum of the air conditioning, the cars in traffic, or the voices of those close by.

As you rein your attention fully into the present, let go of all of your frustrations and worries. Ask yourself, "At this very moment, do I have any problems?" You might say, "Well, yeah. I've got bills to pay, I'm behind on my work, and I'm going through a rough breakup." While these situations are difficult, all of them have either already happened or might happen in the future. For right NOW, at this very moment, what do you have to worry about?

The answer is nothing. You're fine.

"But I'm in debt up to my eyeballs and I'm pretty sure my wife is cheating on me," you might say. Sure. But your "being in debt" is a process that occurred over several months. And your wife cheating on you is something that may or may not have happened – in the past or in the future. These obstacles are simply situations you will need to deal with – and until you do, there is absolutely no point in worrying about them. Let yourself relax and only think about these "problems" when you take action on them. In the mean time, give all you can to the present moment.

Remember this key idea: your thoughts about particular events are what cause you stress and pain – *not the events themselves*. Rather than having your mind run in circles trying to find a solution for something when you have no intention of acting on it at the moment, give it a break. If I were to tell you to stand up right now and do a few jumping jacks, you might look at me funny, but you could do it. However, if I were to tell you to stand up and do a few jumping jacks right now *tomorrow*, you'd look at me in total confusion. Yet this is precisely what your mind tries to do by reaching into the past or the future to solve your problems.

If you can grasp this idea, you can be freed from your mind's tyranny over your consciousness. Understand that it almost always demands to know what's WRONG, what needs FIXING, what's DAMAGED, and what SUCKS in your life. This is because its sole consideration is safety and protection – looking for potential pain and trying to deal with it or avoid it.

Consider this: when was the last time you spent hours contemplating a problem you were facing? You should be able to immediately reach an answer. But when was the last time you spent FIVE minutes contemplating how GREAT something was working in your life? It's shocking how negative our minds can be!

Fortunately, you don't have to identify with these stressful thoughts. In fact, it's not even YOU who creates these thoughts – your mind is just a PART of you. The next time it throws something negative your way that doesn't serve you, observe the thought and its true nature, ask yourself if it's truly empowering you, and then choose another one if it isn't. You have the power to influence your own thinking at any given moment when you discover that you are using your mind instead of it using you.

As Eckhart Tolle beautifully states in his best-selling book, *The Power of Now*, "You are unconsciously identified with it (the mind), so you don't even know that you are its slave. It's almost as if you were possessed without knowing it, and so you take the possessing entity to be yourself. The beginning of freedom is the realization that you are not the possessing entity - the thinker. Knowing this enables you to observe the entity. The moment you start watching the thinker, a higher level of consciousness becomes activated. You then begin to realize that there is a vast realm of intelligence beyond thought, that thought is only a tiny aspect of that intelligence. You also realize that all the things that truly matter - beauty, love, creativity, joy, and inner peace - arise from beyond the mind. You begin to awaken."[26]

Let's explore two powerful ways of enhancing your focus on the present moment and how to recover from situations when you're completely out of it.

Go With the Flow

Going with the flow means accepting the present moment for what it is without judging it as "BAD." This doesn't mean you allow life to dictate itself without your input – being walked over because you refuse to take action. It means that you first accept whatever is happening right now before you, and then taking action if necessary to change it. You go with the flow instead of fighting the stream.

We tend to run from things that cause us pain more than we run towards happiness. Most of the things that we do find pleasurable aren't because they make us happy – they're because we want to avoid pain. We don't watch TV because it makes us feel fulfilled and accomplished; we watch it to avoid boredom. We don't work to pour our passion into something creative; we work to avoid being broke. And for many of us, we get married and have kids not because we want to raise a family, but because we want to avoid being lonely.

This desire to escape from our fears and hide from pain creates resistance. This resistance makes us react to what we don't like – which almost always damages our state of mind, capacity to think clearly, and ability to act authentically. In fact, it is impossible to behave with authenticity if you negatively react to the present moment; you're mentally rejecting your connection to life by responding to what you don't want.

Instead of building up preferences for life and creating a list of the way things "should be," accept things for the way they are. Fully embrace the difficult moments of your life for better or worse. Allow them to exist without trying to run from them, change them, or ignore them. You'll find that there is usually a lesson in dire need of being learned when you face adversity. If you have the courage to fully open up to pain from time to time, you gain insight to profound epiphanies. It is said that discontent is life's most direct way of teaching you.

Without adversity, you won't know what you're fully capable of. You won't be pushed to pull out the most from your skills, talents, and abilities. You will ultimately be cheated from getting to know your deepest power. Don't hate the pain and difficulty you experience throughout life. Instead, understand that all pain serves the necessary purpose of demanding that we become something greater to overcome it. This transformation is a necessary part of your journey.

You can apply this concept to some of life's biggest challenges – whether you're going through divorce, a tough breakup, bankruptcy, being fired from work, or even trying to end a reliance on drugs or alcohol. Face the agony you endure eye-to-eye without blinking and go as deeply into the emotion as possible without resistance. Rather than beating yourself up or lashing out at the world, get as quiet as possible and utilize the opportunity to learn more about who you are. While it can be difficult, accept that the event, which pushed you out of your comfort zone, is actually for your own good. Notice the part of your psyche that demands a stronger version of you to emerge – how it calls attention to your weaknesses and asks you to acknowledge them so you can move past them. Then, rather than dwelling in the negative emotional state, get crystal clear on what you would rather see or have in your life instead. Move forward from that point with the necessary clarity self-awareness brings to avoid repeating the same mistakes later.

Let's look at a more specific example. Picture yourself in a boardroom giving an important presentation. Your job is potentially on the line; if you do not deliver the message properly, you know there will be consequences. Now imagine yourself clicking through your power point information and skipping over an important slide entirely. Your remote has suddenly stopped working and now you're faced with the awkward moment where everyone senses something went wrong. How would you respond?

For many of us (especially those that are terrified of public speaking), making a mistake like this would be catastrophic. A person would probably become embarrassed, chide him or herself for the mistake, and awkwardly attempt to fix the error. They would be *resisting* the present circumstances. You'd see it written all over them: stiff, uncomfortable movements, shallow breathing, sweat pouring down, and a very worried expression on their face. They'd be thinking something like, "This is not happening!" The presentation would probably take a nosedive.

But the reason it would fall apart isn't because of the mistake that person made. It's because of how they *resisted* the situation and chose to *react* to it in a disempowering way. Their confidence would crumble because they weren't comfortable with the new circumstances and panicked. If they would have calmly continued with the presentation or even made a relaxed joke about technology not wanting to behave, they would have been fine.

The lesson here is if you can learn to take situations as they are and roll with them as if nothing is wrong, you are permanently free from mental anguish. Nothing can ever get to you when you recognize everything exists as it's meant to be. Again, this does not mean that you become passive and refrain from exerting willpower into your life. The power in this concept comes from an insistence of thinking, "This is how it is and I'm cool with that" - even if you're going to be taking constructive action to change the circumstances.

If you always go with the flow, you really don't care if someone reacts to you poorly or if things don't go as expected. In fact, doing something that you would consider embarrassing in front of others is remarkably liberating. You will realize that it truly doesn't matter what happens to you in the outer world; how you feel underneath everything is the only thing that matters. When you acknowledge that you are always "fine" in situations you were previously terrified of, you become invincible.

Be looking out for resistance when it shows up in your life. When you're in a situation with the potential for rejection, notice how you tend to pull your punches because the interaction might not go the way you want – how you shield yourself from possible pain by holding back. Catch yourself shying away from these moments and then do precisely the opposite of what you're tempted to do. Go deeper into them – completely embrace the moment and every aspect of it. Accept everything as it happens and take joy in the present moment no matter what unfolds. This type of courage rewards you with flawless confidence.

Breathing

Your breath serves as a constant reminder to be present and connected to life. By giving a heightened attention to your breathing and consciously controlling it, you can quickly return to the present moment and instantly feel relaxed. This is because our emotions are tied into our breathing; when we're nervous, our breaths are shallow and short; when we're angry, we hold onto them; when we're relaxed, they're slow and deep. Similar to how your physiology is tied into your confidence, your breathing directly affects how you feel at any given moment. Any time you change your breathing, you alter your emotional state.

You probably haven't put much thought into your breath before. In fact, I'm fairly positive that you haven't taken more than a few minutes out of your entire life to examine this yet (if you have, congratulations - you're the special exception). The average person completely takes their breath for granted and doesn't consider using it to shift their attention. If you fall under this category, don't worry - we're about to change a few things.

Try this now: put one hand on your chest and another on your abdomen. Take a deep breath in, making sure to really fill your lungs with as much air as possible. As you breathe, ask yourself this: which hand moved the most? If the hand over your chest moved more, I have bad news: you're breathing incorrectly. Most people breathe this way – expanding the chest up, raising the shoulders, and lifting the trap muscles higher. However, by doing this consistently, you actually deliver less oxygen to your lungs. Your breathing becomes too shallow and weak.

Rather than breathing from the chest, breathe in from the diaphragm. Put one hand on your abdomen again and take a deep breath from there instead of your chest. Notice how much more air you can fill your lungs with. Pay attention to how much deeper the breath is, how much more it connects you to the present moment, and how much better it feels altogether. This is how you are meant to breathe; it's how newborn babies do it and how to ensure you get the level of oxygen your body demands.

Inhale each time for three to four seconds and exhale for four to five seconds. As you do, imagine pulling in immense relaxation and pushing out all stress and worry. Do this a few times each day, especially when you need to take a quick two minute break from stress or fatigue. Any time you focus on your breath and direct your consciousness in this way, you regain presence.

If you find yourself particularly stressed out, try inhaling for a five count, holding your breath for a five count, and then exhaling for a five count. Repeat this cycle for five to ten minutes or as long as it takes to fully relax and dissolve the negative thoughts. Think of this is as your go-to move for quieting the mind's chatter and feeling alive again.

Another technique you can utilize with your breathing is by practice the art of Qi Gong. This Eastern technique teaches that in order to reach a state of optimum relaxation, all you have to do is control your body, breathing, and mind simultaneously. Often when we are overly nervous, you'll notice that all three of these areas seem outside of our control: our heart beats too quickly, sweat pours out, we may hyperventilate, and our mind fires an unstoppable barrage of negative thoughts our way. The next time you sense you're feeling especially nervous, use a simple Qi Gong exercise.

Begin by controlling the mind with a short mantra you repeat. You can say it out loud or quietly to yourself – it doesn't really matter. This mantra blocks the hundreds of unnecessary thoughts your mind is trying to communicate. Then regulate your breathing by inhaling and exhaling on a specific count – I like doing everything in five second intervals. Lastly, create a rhythm for your body by repeating a specific movement. These three things increase serotonin activity in your brain and lead to deep relaxation. For example, you can start by quietly saying, "breathe" repeatedly to yourself. Then inhale for, hold, and exhale for five second counts. You can then gently rock back and forth to calm your body. Use whatever combination you feel works for you.

The Ego (A.K.A. The Inner Gremlin)

Let's get clear on one thing before we dive into this concept: I'm not talking about the Western concept of someone having "a big ego." I'm not defining this idea as the obsession a person can have with him or herself. I'm also not referring to Sigmund Freud's structural model of the psyche; the way I wish to describe it has nothing to do with the "id" or "super-ego." I just wanted to make that clear before we start discussing one of the more abstract sections of the book.

Here's how I would define the ego given the content we have covered so far: the ego is the identity constructed by the conditioned mind from a reaction to feedback from the outside world. Rather than an identity that comes from within, it is a mask worn in an attempt to receive appreciation, love, and support from others. The ego is steadily built from the experiences we undergo as children that lead us to forming false beliefs about who we are and what we're capable of. Each time that we interpreted an event growing up as one that damaged our self-esteem, the ego added another layer to itself, fooling us into believing that we're not good enough to exist in the world as we are - that there is an inner void we must seek to fill and protect from being exposed. As soon as this belief becomes implanted into our subconscious, we do all we can to manipulate life into showing up a certain way to avoid pain. This side of you does not acknowledge that you have the power to influence, shape, and ultimately create your true identity and life. It completely ignores your deepest strengths and ability to transcend your problems.

Spiritual teachers and psychologists have called the ego various names - the Shadow Self, The Little Voice, the False Self, and the

Devil – but they all point to the same concept. I call it the Inner Gremlin because I think of it as the weak version of us, toiling away to minimize our own happiness and self-confidence by becoming reliant on outer conditions. Instead of building up healthy self-esteem, genuinely caring for others, and feeling otherwise connected to the world, the Inner Gremlin compares, judges, labels, and separates itself from the world. Because it doesn't think of itself as equal to other people, it often seeks to enhance itself by belittling them or trying to get ahead of them. It's either envious of what people have or critical of what they lack.

When we identify primarily with the ego, we draw our identity from our jobs, relationships, money, sex appeal, and our outer results in life. We use these temporary positions of power to assert our worth and confidence to compensate for the feelings of deep inner lack. We're conditioned to spend our money and use our resources on these "band-aids" that will seemingly enhance our self-image and make us feel better about ourselves. The overwhelming message in our culture is that power is not to be found from within; it must be conquered, discovered, bought, or won in the outer world. You can thank the ego for spreading this lie.

This Inner Gremlin of yours can never have enough, be enough, or do enough. It can never be satisfied or content with what you have as it's always craving MORE - more money, more victories, more resources, more everything. You'll find that even when you finally get what you have been yearning for, your ego will only want to appreciate it for mere minutes before moving onto something bigger and more necessary. The Inner Gremlin is insatiable and never really satisfied.

This ego feels that it's often under attack from others so it does all it can to lash out, react, and defend itself. As Osho examines in his book, *Beyond the Frontier of the Mind*: "This ego comes continuously in conflict with others because every ego is so unconfident about itself. It has to be – it is a false thing. When you don't have anything in your hand and you just think that something is there, then there will be a problem. If somebody says, 'There is nothing,' immediately the fight will start because you also feel that there is nothing. The other makes you aware of the fact...you have to defend because if you don't defend, if you don't become defensive, then where will you be? You will be lost. The identity will be broken."27

Can you see how behaving in this manner is so destructive to your happiness and peace of mind? Can you see how most of your attempts to gain confidence have come from your ego's desperate cry for attention and validation? Most of the needless suffering you experience on a daily basis is related to your mind's quest to satisfy this silly part of you. The bad news is that you're likely going to be grappling with the ego for most of your life; it will show up in subtle ways even when you have done a lot of inner work. The good news is that you always have the power to direct your thoughts in beneficial ways that transcend it.

Let's zoom into a few key strategies for either weakening the Inner Gremlin's reign over your mind or strengthening your ability to bypass it.

Don't Take Your SELF Seriously

You can think of the ego as a hollow shell made of paper mache that might look appealing on the surface but doesn't have the fortitude to hold up under a strong breeze. We carefully craft this thing together, gluing the pulp onto the structure and painting the exterior to showcase our personality to the world. We often hope that this fake version of ourselves won't be challenged or criticized – because if it is, we know it could fall to pieces instantly. So we leap to its defense, either hiding it from attacks or lashing out in anger to back our opponents away.

The ego shapes a lot of your personality, which is derived from the ancient Latin word *persona*, literally translating to "mask." In many ways, your personality is simply the mask you choose to decorate and wear for society. This is your routine method of expression that feels most comfortable to you and most in alignment with your self-image. Behaving contrary to this personality often feels counter to your self-image – almost like you are acting or putting on a performance. This feeling is known as cognitive dissonance – it's the discomfort you experience when trying to behave in ways that oppose your routine social strategies for coping with society.

Ironically, your personality has always been an acting performance. The role you portray is simply the character you feel most comfortable playing based on feedback from others. You may be extremely extroverted because each time you speak your mind others tend to laugh. You may be extremely introverted because someone criticized you for speaking up at one point in your life. You may utilize a sense of humor because you found it to be an excellent coping mechanism. No matter how you think of yourself, most of what defines your personality has to do with how other people could react to you. Whether or not you are consciously aware of it, you created this character and put it on stage in hopes of receiving "a round of applause" (and not boo's) from your audience.

I'm sure you are familiar with the expression 'don't take yourself so seriously.' Here's how I like to say it: ' don't take your SELF so seriously.' Your SELF being the confines of the personality your ego created. If you've ever been presented with an opportunity to do something, and your answer was, "No, I can't do that, that's not me," you have brushed up against the walls of your personality. The more rigid and immovable these walls are, the less confident and at ease you'll feel in new environments and situations.

Imagine your entire personality as an ink splatter against a large map with different zones on it. The majority of the splatter takes up the middle of the map with blobs randomly strewn about the paper. The splatter represents where you feel most confident or "yourself". The parts of the map without any ink on them represent where you feel unconfident or "not yourself." These are the areas you don't feel certain your personality would be comfortable in.

Now imagine that you've just been invited to your boss's toga party. Everyone from work is coming dressed in togas, and if you don't show up, you're going to miss out on hitting it off with your cute co-worker. The problem is, you've never felt comfortable dressing up. Halloween is something you celebrate by leaving a bowl of candy out for the kids and shutting the blinds. What do you do? Do you stay at home and miss out on the fun or do you arrive at the party feeling awkward and out of place?

This is a perfect example of when you need to learn to not take your SELF so seriously and work to expand your blueprint. Show up to the party in spite of feeling awkward and embrace the discomfort as you stretch your personality. Wear the loudest toga there – paint it pink if you can – and shock yourself out of the identity you've carved for yourself over the years. The more you act like this, the more you weaken your ego's attempts at controlling you. You realize that you are bigger than the paper mache mask you wear and that the only limits on your personality are the ones you create.

Look to do things that seem contrary to your personality and behave in ways your ego believes are foolish, pointless, and "not you." Run around your house or apartment, yell, make animal noises, jump up and down, chant, dance, speak with an accent, sing loudly as you run errands - do something you would normally never do out of fear of embarrassment.

Regularly take part in activities that push you out of your comfort zone and expand your inkblot. Hang out with people you wouldn't normally hang out with, eat things you wouldn't normally eat, and go places you wouldn't normally go. Not only will you lead a more fulfilling life, but your self-confidence will rise dramatically as there will be fewer and fewer aspects of life you aren't comfortable with. Remember that you are far more than just the mask you wear – you have the ability to showcase a hundred different sides of you.

Practice Self-Control

The second way to minimize the ego is through self-control – the willpower you exert to control your actions, thoughts, and emotions. If you allow your ego to run freely in your life, you will find laziness, mental chaos, and emotional angst in all that you do. Remember that the natural state of the Inner Gremlin is that of insecurity and lack. It wants to waste all of your mental energy comparing you to other people and struggling to find reasons for you to feel good about yourself. By letting it run wild, you won't have much willpower left over to do anything productive or follow through on what you said you were going to do.

Notice that you will naturally feel great about who you are when you exert self-control. When you workout or exercise regularly, you feel healthy and strong. When you hold a strong posture with your body language, you feel confident and powerful. When you control your speech and use precision language to communicate, you feel more articulate and charismatic. When you direct your actions in alignment with your biggest goals, you feel productive and successful. I could list hundreds of examples.

Conversely, when you lack self-control, consider how poorly you tend to think of yourself. You skip the trip to the gym and you feel lazy. You let your body slump over when someone is speaking with you and you seem lethargic. You stumble through a long-winded explanation and don't feel like the other party understands what you're trying to say. You show up with a lack of discipline and you become frustrated with yourself. Again, I could go on and on.

In Chapter Three, I wrote about the importance of having integrity and why as a man you should absolutely honor your word and keep your commitments. Your ego doesn't see much value in this because there is no drama – showing up on time isn't exciting, following through on what you said you were going to do isn't exhilarating, and doing something when you don't feel like doing it isn't particularly compelling. Here's the deal: your ego doesn't enjoy when you do these things because they *weaken its power over you*.

Let's talk about James Dean for a second. He is universally acknowledged as one of the coolest guys to ever grace the planet. Watching his films gives a person the opportunity to study him – to check out his moves, the way he holds his posture, and to hear him speak. Think about how much self-control he exerts in these movies; there are no unnecessary gestures or wasted movements. He consciously leans against objects in his environment, he speaks slowly and with a controlled measure, he smiles in unexpected ways that seem to fall entirely on his own terms, and there's no nervous fidgeting or needless rambling. He expresses just enough to get his points across with a balanced, controlled energy and then unleashes a surge of emotional intensity when important scenes call for it. He had an uncanny ability to transition from a relaxed nonchalance to a passionate outburst in seconds.

Having a high-level of self-control affords you the ability to exert power. Practice the James Dean body language and control how you move and take up space. Practice discipline by repeatedly following through on your commitments and forming healthy habits. Practice expanding your comfort zone by doing things that scare you. As you face resistance from your ego, keep moving forward in spite of feelings of discomfort. The uncomfortable friction you experience will weaken over time and you will be able to behave in alignment with your true self. The power comes from dictating your behaviors on your terms – an expression that isn't limited by what society would appreciate or what you've shown in the past. The more self-control you have, the more opportunities you have to evolve and shed layers of the ego.

9

CREATE YOUR CODE

"It is through the understanding of ourselves that fear comes to an end." – Krishnamurti

This is it – you've made it to the last chapter. My hope is that you've been able to make several key distinctions about your relationship with you and the world. If you zoom out and think big picture, my goal is to ultimately shift your mindset from a reliance on the approval of others to an undeniable sense of self-trust. Back in chapter two we took a closer look at what social conditioning is - and how essentially you were programmed to believe that inner-confidence doesn't exist from a very young age – that you must buy it, make enough money to be worth it, or follow what society said was important for you to receive it. Many men never grow out of these childish beliefs and think they must win over the approval of others in order to be happy.

Fortunately, you don't have to fall victim to this fallacy. You're going to be creating your code – a life designed according to your highest values, goals, and aspirations. This code serves as the framework for your identity and will be something you can come back to as a reference point and build upon time and time again. You're going to be more intimately aware of the kind of man you are now and want to become. You're charting out your own road map with a more accurate perception of who you REALLY are and what you REALLY want in life. This entire chapter serves to give you some powerful tools to ignoring social pressure and becoming your own man with unshakable confidence.

You're about to learn:

- How to define what you value and what matters most to you, regardless of what society deems important

- What your core message is and the power you can access from it

- How to release all the emotional blocks in your way to free up your energy

- How to discover a natural confidence that stems from honoring your greatest passions and gifts

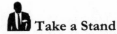 Take a Stand

If you were to take a camera and a microphone and head to your nearest city to interview men as they walked by, and you simply asked them, "What do you value most in your life?" most of the answers would sound like:

"Uhhh I don't know"

"My family"

"Umm good times with friends"

"Hot women!"

"A good job"

In fact, I believe plugging these answers into a game of Family Feud would make guessing the top five answers a breeze. Your team would come up with everything in a matter of seconds. Most guys have very little idea about what is important to them, and when they do know, it almost always concerns areas they have put very little thought into. They have a good understanding of what they WANT but know very little about WHO they want to BE. Look, I'm not saying that friends, family, and hot women aren't important. I'm just saying these are "gimmes" - they're obvious choices that don't reflect any true inner clarity.

My challenge for you is to go beyond these obvious clichés by defining what you stand for. What beliefs, ideas, mindsets, and aspects of life are important to you and exemplify who you are? What will you wave a flag for and plant in the soil for others to rally around?

Alexander Hamilton famously said, "If you don't stand for something, you'll fall for anything." If you don't possess clear-cut values, your life won't have a clear direction. You'll hesitate when faced with dilemmas, be an easier target for manipulation, and generally drift through daily activities. You'll often feel like you don't have a true purpose and will react more to social pressure than your own intuition. Conversely, when you have firm values in place, making decisions becomes far easier. You will second-guess yourself far less often and take action with bold confidence. Others will respect the fire they see in your eyes compared to the men who aimlessly wander without direction.

In order to get clear on what you stand for, you need to set aside some time to commit these values to paper. Before you move on past this section, set aside at least half an hour to completely focus. Turn off your cell phone, eliminate any potential distractions, and allow yourself the opportunity to think and meditate. This period of quiet isolation will allow you to clearly identify what you stand for and what is truly important to you – and remember, clarity is power. The more specific and clear you are with these values, the more you will gain from the exercise.

Understand that this time of self-reflection isn't going to be easy. Sitting down and considering your values is quite frankly the last thing your ego or conditioned mind want you to do. Be prepared for a wide range of emotions – everything from writer's block, boredom, and anxiety to show up. There's a reason most people don't have the courage or willingness to look inside of themselves; this exercise is designed to stretch you.

This is why you must be willing to go in DEEP. If you cheat yourself out of this exercise, you're cheating yourself out of your own power. You're building a foundation right now, and ignoring these steps is akin to chopping off one of the legs on a table. DO NOT read any further until you have finished this.

Found somewhere quiet and have at least thirty minutes free? Good - take out a pen and some paper and write down your answers to these questions. Take your time with them and don't hesitate to revisit these often.

1. **Who are you? What roles do you play in your life and to whom?**

    Think about who influences you the most - who you care about deeply and respect. Also consider whom you influence the most as well. How do you affect those closest to you?

2. **How do you see yourself when you're at your best?**

    Think about those times in your life when everything is clicking. What kinds of activities are you taking part in? Who are you with? What kind of thoughts are running through your head? What does your personality feel like during these moments? Focus on all the ways you would describe yourself when you are "in the zone."

3. **What ideas, traits, or characteristics do you value most? Write down everything that comes to mind.**

    Some examples are: courage, imagination, fun, hope, happiness, love, leadership, freedom, integrity, responsibility, service, wisdom, God, spirituality, clarity, growth, intelligence, loyalty, balance, health, etc. Think about the ethics, principles, morals, or beliefs you stand

218

for that have guided your life up until this point or could guide you in the future.

4. **Out of the values you just listed, circle the top five. How do you embody these values daily?**

Think about why you chose these top five values. What makes them more important than the others? Why did you choose them and how has your life reflected this choice? Meditate on how your identity has been shaped by them.

5. **What are you absolutely not willing to tolerate from others? What values will you not accept being broken, either by yourself or by someone else?**

This question is vitally important for you to know so that you can stand in your power. It's crucial to know when to put up your shield and block negative people and thoughts from entering your psyche. If you tolerate everything, you won't have a firm identity that makes you unique and sets you apart from others. Put some deep thought into answering this.

6. **What is your purpose in life? What would you like people to say about you when you're gone?**

What is the one thing you believe you were born to accomplish? What are you so passionate about and gifted with that doing it is easy and almost effortless? Continue expanding your vision for your life. What do you want your lasting legacy to be?

7. **What values or beliefs are you willing to die for? What matters so much to you that life would not be worth living without?**

For example, if you value love the most, and suddenly the world became devoid of love, how would you feel? What would you do to get back the single most important thing to you? Again, reflect on your answer and put some deep thought into it.

These values will continuously evolve and shift over time. Don't feel pressured to perfect everything right now; it's an ongoing process that will change as you change. Keep in mind the questions you have answered are not designed to be easy. They are meant to challenge your mind to access the strongest and deepest ways of defining who you are. In order to properly answer them, you must dig deep under the superficial to get to what truly constitutes you. If you're not satisfied with any of your answers, it's OK. Take a walk, think about the questions in your spare time, and let the values come to you.

Keep what you have written down in a safe place or transfer it to a document on your computer if you can. You want to be able to access these often to remind you about what you stand for; they are a huge part of your foundation that can guide you in times of tough decisions. To take this concept even farther, pin your top five values up somewhere near your desk (whichever one you use the most). This serves as a constant reminder of what you stand for and who you are at your greatest.

Your Core Message

Now that you have your values in place, you can begin to create your core message. This is your one key belief that embodies who you are and what you stand for. It's a quick sentence or two that sums up your unique perspective of life. By articulating your core message, you plant your flag in the ground and choose how you wish to be defined rather than blindly following someone else's beliefs. With this prepared, you can easily identify people in your life who don't support your perspective and who you should not waste much time with rather than seeking everyone's approval.

Flip to another clean sheet of paper and take a second to answer these questions:

1. **What makes you different from others? What separates you from the herd?**

Consider what beliefs you have that differ from your typical guy. Think about the roles you play in your life again. How do you play a specific role differently than someone else in your shoes would?

2. What do you believe to be true about life?

What global beliefs do you have about life? How does a person find success, happiness, and strength? What is the most important thing you have ever learned?

3. What do you believe to be true about you?

What kind of man are you? What kind of reputation would you like to have with others? What kind of reputation would you outright reject?

Once you've put some thought into these questions, you can start to develop your core message. Pick out some of your favorite answers, circle them, and then mix and match what feels the best. Here are a few examples:

"I believe we all have the capacity to evolve into someone a weaker version of us would never recognize."

"What makes a man great isn't his ability to find success but his willingness to actively seek opportunities for failure so he can learn, grow, and improve."

"Life is the hell you make it and the heaven you take it as. We create everything that happens to us."

"We don't get what we want. We get what we are."

"I'm not ever satisfied with just being 'good' at something. I will do whatever it takes to become great, and I only tolerate greatness from others."

You're probably going to come up with several of these statements. Keep refining your favorite until you feel like it really defines who you are and what you believe in. Remember that your goal is to take a stand for something – to draw a line in the sand that is meant to turn some people away. That's not to say that you shouldn't be open to new perspectives and opinions; you can always learn from those who think differently. However, a core message affords you the clarity to say NO to the people you need to in order to preserve your integrity.

By design, this core expression isn't meant to be welcomed or appreciated by everyone. There will always be those who don't agree with your viewpoint and will even outright vilify it. But this doesn't matter. Your goal isn't to win everyone over. Your goal is to find your core audience and share with them what they need to hear: your story, your knowledge, your talents, and your encouragement. Rather than trying to defend your message or fighting with those who disparage you, ignore them. There are thousands who gravely need your attention instead.

Right now you might not feel like you have much influence in the world, but keep in mind that every movement starts small. There is probably ONE person in your life right now who could benefit from your perspective. Rather than deluding yourself into believing you're not "good enough" yet to share what you know, start giving your gifts to someone who could benefit from them the most. I don't care how far along the spectrum of success you think you are – whether you're a millionaire or a student struggling to pay the bills, you have something to offer because you will always have more experience than those who want to accomplish what you have. Allow your core message to broadcast your talents and viewpoints to the world and don't hesitate to help those who might need your attention.

 Your Personal Evolution

The next step in creating your code is being clear about the direction you want to go in life and who you want to become. To do that, it's vitally important to not only maintain a clear vision for the characteristics you want to embody, but also to let go of toxic emotions and limiting beliefs that have been holding you back. If you can focus your attention on the type of life you want to live while simultaneously shutting down the energy you give to your inner-negativity, you can kill two huge birds with one stone.

Throughout every person's life, they are either growing by expanding their self-concept and living into new empowering beliefs or they are dying by either repeating a disempowering story about why they can't have what they want or harboring destructive emotions. Remember that your mind can only focus on one thing at a time – choose to evolve and move on from the past.

Design Your Ideal Self

The more clarity you have about the man you want to evolve into, the more likely it is that over time, you will assume his identity. This process begins with having a detailed and well-thought out vision of who you want to become and then choosing to embrace those characteristics as often as possible.

Find somewhere quiet again and take a few minutes to answer these questions:

1. **Describe in detail your ideal self in the present tense.**

   How do you look? How do you sound? How do you feel day to day? What are you thinking about? How do you dress? What types of friends do you have? Do you have a sense of humor or are you mellower? Act as if you have all of these qualities now and put them to paper.

2. **What are your confidence goals?**

   In other words, what powers, capabilities, and characteristics do you want to have? Write these down in present tense as well. Here are some examples: I can talk to anyone anywhere, I am the life of the party everywhere I go, I am extremely confident giving presentations and speeches, etc.

3. **Imagine the most nerve-racking experience possible for you, something your former self would cower from and suffer immense pain from encountering. Write down how your ideal self handles that situation with ease.**

   For example, if you're terrified of giving speeches or speaking in front of others, imagine the worst possible scenario. Maybe you realize you forgot your notes and are due on stage in two minutes. What do you do? How does your ideal self handle it?

4. **Who do you need to become so you can die complete? Who must you be to feel like your purpose has been accomplished?**

Think about what you would like to achieve, but spend most of your time focused on the characteristics and personality traits you want to acquire or build on.

Knowing exactly the kind of man you want to become, how you would handle key decisions, and what goals you'd like to work towards are extremely powerful. The very act of committing them to paper etches them into your subconscious. This is vastly more beneficial than just vaguely thinking or daydreaming about them. This is you getting definite about your growth and fulfilling your intentions. Again, this process is not designed to be easy, and I realize I'm making you work more in this chapter, but every minute you spend investing your time with this builds your inner-strength.

Before you move onto the next session, take a ten-minute break and visualize an important meeting. After you read this, close your eyes and imagine meeting your ideal self one on one. This is the version of you that has achieved, become, and lived the life you have always wanted to live.

As he walks up to shake your hand, picture the clothes he's wearing. Does he wear a suit or something more casual? How does his outer image reflect his personality? Imagine his character and how he relates to the world. Does he have a great sense of humor? Is he serious and focused? How confident is he? Gather some distinct details of this person as you meet him.

Then have him take you on a guided tour of your future life. Have him show you exactly what you do as part of your daily routine: the time you wake up in the morning, the breakfast you eat, the work you do for a living that is designed to best suit your passions and talents, the people you associate with, and the fun you enjoy in your free time. Do you have a family with kids running around the house? Are you an eligible bachelor? Have your kids grown up and moved on, leaving you and your wife a chance to grow closer?

After spending some time in your future life, return to the present and ask your ideal self a simple question: "what do I need to do in order to receive the life I dream of?" Recognize that whatever he tells you, no matter how much or how little, is exactly what you need to hear. Respect his advice and take concentrated action on this suggestion.

You can utilize this powerful visualization whenever you want to; in fact the more you imagine this ideal version of you, the better. If you're unable at first to clearly see the future version of you, connect more with the emotions of what it feels like to experience life as him. Let your intuition guide you without trying to think too much – your subconscious knows far more than your conscious mind will let you believe.

In looking forward to the man you want to become, you might notice some of the things he values are different than what you currently value. Similarly, you might be aware of a gap between what you think is important now and what he will ultimately view as important. If it helps, go back and update your values to reflect your future vision. For example, you might value hard work right now, but when you visualize your ideal self, you see him relaxing and enjoying life more often. So you might want to think about adding balance to your list of values – even if you feel like your life is mostly about working hard right now.

In addition, be thinking about how you will hold yourself accountable to following through on the values your ideal self embodies. What will you do to ensure that you stay committed to your principles? Try to anticipate some potential obstacles and jot them down so you're well equipped to handle them.

Forgive and Forget

One of the biggest barriers between you and achieving success in any calling is the amount of emotional clutter you still carry with you. If you have any feelings of anger, guilt or sadness still residing in you based on what happened to you in the past, you will have a far more difficult time getting what you want. This is because your emotional baggage blocks what you want to receive in your life and weighs heavily on what you want to create.

You can't have one hand outstretched for the future with one holding onto the past and expect to go anywhere – this is akin to a car screeching down the street with the emergency brake on. When you harbor negative emotions inside you, they rob you of your confidence and wellbeing by eating away at your energy and mood. Your willpower depletes far more rapidly, your mind cannot think as clearly, and you leave very little mental space available for focusing on what you want to create. The more emotional clutter you have, the more difficulty you're going to find evolving into a healthier person.

I understand if you have been hurt to such a degree that you believe forgiving someone is out of the question. But understand that the less you're willing to let go of the past, the less energy and influence you can have in the future. This is a choice you're going to have to make: is the pain you're still holding onto TRULY serving you or is it time to let it go?

Buddha said, "Holding onto anger is like grasping a hot coal with the intent of throwing it at someone else; you are the one getting burned." We often think that by forgiving someone we're admitting they were right to act the way they did to us. We want to keep feeling angry or upset with someone long after the event has passed because it can give us a sense of self-righteousness. Our ego loves feeding off of the "I'm right about this and they are clearly wrong" mindset. But consider this: the other person isn't the one suffering from your decision to stay in the past. *You* are the only one experiencing this pain. You don't have to admit the other person was "right" - in fact you can still go on believing that YOU were RIGHT all along – but you must choose to forgive them.

Right now think of one person from your past who you believe has hurt you on some level. Perhaps they were a former business partner who cheated you out of a lucrative deal. Your father might have treated you poorly or may have been too hard on you growing up. Maybe your heart was broken years ago with a difficult divorce or break-up that left you scattered and devastated. You shouldn't have to think too hard about this; we usually have at least one or two painful memories sitting with us that we have a difficult time releasing.

Take a minute or so to clearly select whom you're upset with. Keep in mind the person may be YOU – whomever you're the most angry or upset with is whom you should go with. Don't move on until you have decided.

Once you have selected this person, recreate the specific situation that has caused you harm. Recall the circumstances leading up to the event, who all was involved, and what you were going through at the time. Instead of trying to intellectualize the moment by analyzing it, step into the emotions you felt at the time. Embrace these emotions for as long as it takes until you are feeling them again. If going through the experience with this person made you angry, then allow yourself to feel pissed off. If going through it made you feel sad, then allow yourself to feel somber. Do your best to recreate your emotions in the present moment.

As you experience these feelings again, ask yourself if you want to continue holding onto this pain any longer. Ask yourself if it is truly serving you or if it is time to move on. When you are ready, imagine the pain as a physical entity inside of your body. Visualize the location, size, shape, and color of it as if it was a tangible object. Describe what it looks like - do your best to SEE it inside of you. Even if nothing is really coming to mind, ask yourself, "What *would* it look like?"

Take three deep breaths, inhaling on a five count, holding for a five count, and then exhaling for a five count. When you're ready, imagine this object you described – really visualizing its color, size, and shape - leaving your body. As it moves outside of you, cup your hands around it and hold onto it.

With the object in your hands, simply say, "I now release my feelings of _____ (anger/sadness/fear/jealousy, etc.) and completely forgive what happened." As soon as you say this, take your hands and mentally crush the object to pieces until it turns into a fine powder and then drop the dust onto the floor. If you feel like the emotion is still there, repeat the process as many times as necessary to eliminate it.

Taking just five minutes a day to practice forgiveness in this manner will make an immediate shift to your state of mind. You'll feel lighter, happier, and more balanced the more you take time to do this. However, keep in mind that your ego is NOT going to enjoy this. Your ego (if it hasn't already) is going to tell you things like, "Well this is corny, it shouldn't be this easy to stop feeling negative emotions, and I don't even think it's going to work." Just recognize that by practicing forgiveness, you're making conscious strides to once again override your ego's control over you and it may very well want to fight this process. If you feel any resistance towards practicing forgiveness, just remember to ask yourself this simple question: "Do I like feeling this way?" If the answer is no, then give yourself the freedom to release the toxic emotion.

If you want to take it a step further, ask yourself, "How am I grateful this person or situation came into my life? What has he/she/it taught me?" Even if you feel there is really nothing coming up, imagine what it *could be*. In this sense, you further realize that everyone on this planet serves you in some way. In our greatest challenges, a lesson is always there to be learned. So choose to learn it!

As mentioned before, you might be most upset with yourself. Maybe you came up short, made a critical mistake, or did something you have regretted ever since. As important as it is to forgive other people who you believe have hurt you, it is crucial and necessary to forgive yourself. With how much pressure we were under as kids to maintain good grades, make sound decisions, and find success in this world, we often interpreted our own mistakes and failures as unforgivable sins. Worse yet, many of us believe we should be punished for these mistakes on an ongoing, never-ending basis for falling short of our ideals. If this sounds like you, I suggest you drop this habit of beating yourself up completely. Entirely forgive yourself for any slip-ups you might have made, wipe the slate clean, and move on. You are not serving anyone by harboring a grudge against yourself.

If you would like to pursue an even greater depth of emotional forgiveness, I highly recommend *The Sedona Method* by Hale Dwoskin. You can find his website at http://www.sedona.com.[28]

Demolish the Story

Think back to chapter one when we discussed what your story is – the main limiting belief you have that blocks you from getting what you want. In case you're foggy with the details, your story sounds something like: "I'm not good enough, I'm not smart enough, I'm too young, I'm too old, I'm not capable, I'm not worthy of success, I'll never get what I want, I'm not important, etc." From reading this book so far, hopefully you have already eliminated some negative beliefs or at the very least have reconsidered their power over you.

What we're going to do now is simply take a global belief survey to gauge how truly confident you currently feel. After rating yourself 1-10 with each of the following beliefs, you should get an immediate idea of what your biggest story or limiting belief is. With this information in place, we will then look at an effective method for removing it so that you are free to completely express who you are.

On a scale of 1-10, with one feeling not true at all to you, and ten feeling absolutely true, rate how much you believe the following statements about yourself:

1. I'll never get what I want (__/10)

2. I'm not good enough (__/10)

3. I'm not valuable to others (__/10)

4. What I have to say doesn't matter (__/10)

5. People don't respect me (__/10)

6. I'm not a strong leader (__/10)

7. I don't have much influence with others (__/10)

8. I can't handle rejection (__/10)

9. I can't handle criticism (__/10)

10. I'm boring (__/10)

11. I'm a failure (__/10)

12. I care what people think about me (__/10)

13. I'm not comfortable being myself (__/10)

14. I'm easily intimidated (__/10)

15. I change my personality so I'm accepted by others (__/10)

16. I don't have what it takes to succeed (__/10)

17. I'm not worthy of happiness (__/10)

18. I struggle setting firm boundaries (__/10)

19. I don't like what I see in the mirror (__/10)

20. I don't really have a clear direction in life (__/10)

21. I mentally beat myself up a lot (__/10)

22. I'm afraid of taking risks (__/10)

23. I hesitate to speak my mind (__/10)

24. I'm not very decisive (__/10)

25. I'm not very motivated (__/10)

26. I'm too self-conscious (__/10)

27. I fail to live up to my own standards (__/10)

28. I have a tough time relaxing (__/10)

29. I'm not very smart (__/10)

30. I tend to reject compliments (__/10)

Now scan the list of these thirty beliefs and circle your top five with the highest score. These are the mindsets you have right now that challenge your confidence the most. Once you are clear on the top five, pick one that you feel resonates the most with you. This might be a variation of your story you have already chosen or it may be something completely different. Pick the one belief that feels the most true for you right now in your life.

Now think back to where you believe the negative belief came from. Try to find its source. I'm willing to bet it came from your childhood — somewhere between the ages of six to ten years old. At this age, our parents' expectations for us become higher and failing to meet them can cause damage to our self-esteem. Because as children we don't know that our minds are solely responsible for attaching meaning to events, we mistakenly believe that the events themselves contain meaning. We subconsciously reach conclusions like, "My Dad is yelling at me for screwing up in Math — that must mean I'm not good enough" and unfortunately carry these stories with us throughout our entire lives. Because we never knew we consciously created them, we also never directly challenge them.

Take a look at your strongest limiting belief again and take some time to reflect back to where it came from. More than likely, it originated from an experience that concerned your parents, although something at school might have triggered it as well. When do you think you believed this story for the first time? If you can't recall a specific event, think back to a pattern or a series of events that occurred that led you to feel this way.

With the source of the belief in mind, take a minute to now visualize yourself as a kid going through the experience again. See everyone involved, picture what happened to the best of your abilities, and see yourself reaching the negative conclusion about who you are. Replay the event a few times in your mind so you can see and feel it clearly.

Now what I want you to do is to again visualize the exact same event as a kid — but this time picture your ideal self standing next to you. This is the version of you that not only knows how and why you created this disempowering belief, but also has tons of evidence for why it's simply not true. As the event plays out this time, have your ideal self speak to you as a child. Hear him give you a *different* meaning or interpretation of the event. Perhaps he says, "Your parents expectations of you weren't met in this specific instance, but it doesn't mean that you are _____ (insert story here)." Or he could put his hand on your shoulder and say, "This had nothing to do with you, but everything to do with your parents." Maybe he kneels down next to you and says, "The belief that _____(insert your story) might have been true for you as a kid, but that doesn't mean it has to be true any more."

Choose a new interpretation for the event you experienced as a child that you feel the most confident with. Remember that nothing has any inherent meaning until your brain assigns it meaning – and you can always give new meaning to previous moments, even if they occurred years ago.

For example, perhaps your strongest story is "What I have to say doesn't matter." When you think back to your childhood, you recall an instance when you were seven years old and won a major award at school. You were extremely excited to tell your father about it, but he told you to be quiet and to leave him alone so he could relax. At the time, you took this experience to mean, "What I have to say doesn't matter" and internalized it as true. Revisiting this moment with your ideal self, you picture him telling you, "Your Father was extremely tired at this time and did not have the energy to give really anyone much attention. I'm sure if you would have shared the news with him at a different time, he would have been excited to hear it. In fact, I'm sure he was really proud of you but just didn't have the enthusiasm to show it."

With a new meaning in place, you're going to again visualize meeting your ideal self – except this time as your current age. Picture yourself telling him, "I used to believe that event meant _____ (insert limiting story), and now I want to believe that _____ (insert the opposite of this belief). I need some evidence to help me support this claim." Then imagine him giving you four reasons why you should believe the OPPOSITE of your disempowering belief. Think about every moment in your life where you can either tear down your previous story or build up its replacement with supporting proof.

For example, continuing with "What I have to say doesn't matter," you would tell your ideal self, "I used to believe that when my Father ignored me, it meant that what I have to say doesn't matter. Now I want to believe that everything I want to express is valuable and important for others to hear. I need some evidence to help me support this claim." Your ideal self could then say, "Well, I have four moments in time that completely verify your new belief. They are:

- When you were twenty years old and gave advice to your brother regarding what to focus on in college. He followed your suggestions to the letter and graduated with a degree in film, something he's very passionate about and loves doing to this day. He wouldn't be in this situation without you.

- The time you coordinated a vacation with some co-workers and designed almost everything your group did together. Everyone that went had a great time.

- When you gave the eulogy at your grandfather's funeral and received appreciation and praise from several members of your family for delivering an incredible speech.

- The time you successfully negotiated the cost of your newest car and almost walked out on the salesman several times until you got the price you wanted.

You can choose any moment from your life to help support your new belief, whether it occurred yesterday or back when you were a kid. After you visualize your ideal self giving you four new pieces of evidence, take a deep breath and say your #1 limiting belief out loud again. Take another deep breath and then say the opposite of this belief out loud. Feel out which one feels more true to you. Hopefully, your new thought is more powerful at this point than your old story. If it's not, then go back through this process – you might need to choose a different source or point in time the belief generated from or you might want to select a different meaning for it altogether.

Repeat this process with each of your four remaining beliefs you previously selected. If you want to REALLY dig out your mental blockages, repeat these steps with ten of your limiting beliefs or until none of the thirty statements rate higher than a five for you.

This process of eliminating limiting beliefs was partly inspired by Morty Lefkoe's work. If you are interested in diving deeper into this type of process, I suggest visiting his website: http://www.mortylefkoe.com.[29]

Lastly, remember the tools I gave you in chapter seven for launching into an empowering emotional state. Use visualization to imagine yourself embodying your new beliefs and see yourself abandoning old stories that no longer serve you. Utilize affirmations to reprogram your subconscious mind on a daily basis to lock these new beliefs into place and make them feel more real to you.

 Your Natural Path

This is the last section of the book. If you've made it this far, I want to acknowledge your hunger and drive for serious inner-growth. I might be wrong, but I imagine most of those who picked up this book stopped reading several chapters ago. That's not so much a negative comment about the quality of my book (I obviously hope this has offered you several new perspectives and tools for upgrading your life) – but more so a comment on the habits of people in general. Ironically, we tend to get a sense of exactly what is stopping us, see what is necessary to overcome it, make a little bit of progress, and then stop altogether. Going the distance and finishing what we start doesn't seem to be taken as seriously in our culture. After all, the extra mile is never crowded.

I point this out because the final piece of Unshakable Swagger is precisely about going the extra mile. It's about having the courage to follow your unique path and honoring what makes you most happy. This is arguably the most difficult knowledge to apply to a person's life given the pressures we experience from society to

234

conform and fulfill expectations. However, honoring one's Natural Path is the key to a rich and rewarding journey. It is how one accesses the greatest version of himself in a way that cannot be defeated or disregarded by another man.

What you have read so far has built up to this point. It is my goal for you to take the previously mentioned tools and strategies to heart so that you can follow your Natural Path. If you are able to truly honor it – to live your life in a way that calls to your spirit, I will be grateful to have shared this experience with you.

What is the Natural Path?

Throughout this book, I have planted a few questions or comments that hinted at uncovering your Natural Path. Just a few pages ago, we took an in-depth look at your values and who you wanted your ideal self to be. When I asked you what your purpose was in life, I hinted at this idea. When you expressed your core message, you uncovered a chunk of what it's about. In fact, beginning the book in chapter one by defining what Unshakable Swagger *isn't*, I essentially laid out the greatest delusions that take you away from following this path. You're already more familiar with this concept than you think.

Your Natural Path is made of two parts: the discovery of your natural skills, talents, and passions and a generous expression of these gifts to the world. In following Your Natural Path, you fulfill your purpose in life, recognize the impact you are meant to have, and honor your intuition and highest vision for yourself. Put succinctly, it is who you are meant to be.

In Laurence Boldt's *Tao of Abundance*, the author describes this process as living in accordance with your *Te* or innate power. When a man lives a life that is not in harmony with it, he tends to feel weaker: "Your nature is your strength. To deny it is to rob yourself of your own power...many deny their talents, gifts, and abilities, then complain they can't be happy or successful in this world. This is like placing leg-irons around your ankles and then complaining that you can't run fast. Following your nature is a simple matter of doing what you're naturally good at."[30]

The number one obstacle to following your Natural Path is your ego. Rather than possessing the confidence to respect your true purpose, it believes you must do what is necessary to gain approval. It thinks you need to prove you are worthy of love and appreciation from the world, and so it attempts to coerce you into playing society's games to conform and find acceptance. Rather than trusting you to find peace with your work, it assumes your work isn't sufficient unless enough people think it is valuable. Your ego does its best to design your entire life's journey according to the wishes of others, not once checking in with you to verify if the choices you are making are even moving you closer to what you really want.

To overcome this delusion, realize that you actually don't have anything to prove. Instead of trying to win over society's acceptance, simply follow Your Natural Path, which is paved with your unique aspirations, talents, and gifts. Discover the power inherent in aligning with what you are truly meant to do and let that fuel your confidence rather than basing it on the opinion of others.

How to Discover Your Natural Path

Discovering Your Natural Path is anything but easy. As Joseph Campbell said, "Social pressure is the enemy! I've seen it happen. How in heaven's name are you going to find your own track if you are always doing what society tells you to do?" For many of us, our parents laid down a specific set of expectations that influenced our decision making (and probably still influences to this day). Even if your parents supported you in following your passions, they more than likely wanted you to follow them in a particular way. At some point or another, we have all faced pressure from our family to live into a predetermined vision of our future.

The rest of society also played a role in this too – remember what we discussed in chapter two regarding social conditioning. Through repetitive advertising, the media conditions us to use monetary status to buy happiness – not to look within for it. Through punishment and negative reinforcement, the school system conditions us to avoid failure and mistakes by following a cookie-cutter process: get "good" grades, get into a "good" college, and then get a "good" job. We encounter very few sources of inspiration to harness and channel our natural gifts.

Because discovering your gifts and talents is rarely going to be handed to you on a silver platter, you must work to uncover them. You must be emphatically independent, willing to go against the good will of your friends and family who might not fully support your inner vision. Rather than seeking feedback from the outer world, you must look inward, utilizing your intuition as a gut check to measure your progress. This is exactly what Apple visionary Steve Jobs pointed out in his 2005 Stanford Commencement Address:

"Your time is limited, so don't waste it living someone else's life. Don't be trapped by dogma – which is living with the results of other people's thinking. Don't let the noise of other's opinions drown out your own inner voice. And most important, have the courage to follow your heart and intuition. They somehow already know what you truly want to become. Everything else is secondary."

Finding your Natural Path may take years – you must be willing to shed layers of work and hobbies that move you closer to it but don't necessarily comprise it. As you grow and evolve, your dreams grow and evolve simultaneously. What you were passionate about last year may not interest you nearly as much this year. While this is terrifying to most men who assume something is "wrong with them," take it as a sign that you are moving closer to unlocking your true purpose. In fact, if your passions *don't* change over time, you are more than likely staying in your comfort zone and not taking any steps forward in personal growth.

For example, you might have a job right now as an accountant but play guitar as a hobby. If you could get paid all day long to simply play the guitar, you would – you truly enjoy the activity. However, your work as an accountant is not fulfilling and merely pays your bills. You decide to take a few strides outside of your comfort zone, signing up for Toast Masters to refine your speaking skills. You learn how to effectively communicate in front of a group of people and gain confidence sharing your ideas. You then begin a Youtube channel teaching the world how to play guitar in your spare time and gain momentum from thousands of new subscribers following your content. One day, a business owner reaches out to you and asks you to speak to his employees and train them on social media marketing. You agree, and after giving a great presentation, build a custom keynote presentation you can deliver to any company interested. You book several gigs, quit your job as an accountant, and become a full-time social media expert within a year. Not bad for an accountant, right?

Yes, I realize that this example isn't the most *realistic* probability. However, following your Natural Path often means abandoning the shackles of what "realistic" is altogether. There is nothing realistic about honoring your intuition because what is realistic to society has nothing to do with your own unique journey. From now on, any time someone tells you to be realistic, realize that they are simply trying to coerce you into living according to THEIR values. You and you alone decide what choices are appropriate in life.

With that being said, I want to make it very clear that I am NOT suggesting you quit your day job right at this very moment and go full-time with what you are currently passionate about. Understand that living according to your Natural Path is a steady TRANSITION – not something that happens all at once. While you have a steady paycheck in place, look at ways to maximize your free time when you're not working. Sign up for seminars that teach you new skills. Read new books and listen to new audio on self-development. Attend networking events with people already successful in the field you would like to become an expert in. Continuously invest your time and money in ways to nurture Your Natural Path and consider your job as something that merely funds your research. You may need to try out various avenues before you connect with your greatest passions and talents, however once you locate them, you will know immediately.

The greatest challenge for a person following their path is overcoming the need for an immediate return on investment. If you currently make a living by putting time into a company and then receiving a paycheck every few weeks, you have become conditioned to seeing consistent rewards for your work. Your mind expects to be compensated like clockwork for your daily efforts.

This expectation psychologically hinders your patience and willingness to give your all to the world.

When a man begins to share his talents and skills, he tends to feel an *overwhelming need to be rewarded for his effort*. Stay with me here – this is really critical. If he senses that he is investing time and energy into something that isn't seeing an immediate return on investment (like people buying from him), he wants to HOLD BACK and give LESS until he gets what he wants. To him, the act of giving value without receiving value in return ISN'T FAIR – and this need to have "fairness" stunts his willingness to invest more time, energy, and/or effort into his vision.

This throws a wrench into our ability to generously give value, which is why most people don't pursue their dreams for longer than a few years. Rather than increasing the level of value we provide, we hold it back until we feel like we receive enough in return. When we sense that we're not getting our "fair share," we disengage and stop looking to aggressively share our gifts. This lack of patience and faith in receiving our reward then weakens our connection to our Natural Path, leading us astray and into a place of self-doubt.

Overcoming this challenge is simple: GIVE far more than you will ever expect to receive. Be abundantly generous with sharing your gifts – serve as many people as you can starting right now without expecting anything in return. Start small with those in your life that could benefit from your talents and knowledge. Help them with their problems by coaching them, teaching them, and showing them how to receive the results they want. Begin a podcast, blog, or Youtube channel dedicated to sharing what you know for free. Create a product or service you can give away for free that is worth at least $50. Don't put any thought into how you're "going to make money" off your plan just yet – TRUST that the money will come and will be far beyond what you could possibly imagine.

You will discover your Natural Path as a result of paying close attention to the specific problems you solve as a byproduct of sharing your gifts. In fact, the more you concentrate on the needs of others and the more you LISTEN to what they say they are looking for, the faster you will access your true purpose in life.

After all, your Natural Path is not only designed with *your* happiness in mind, it's designed for the happiness of those who connect with your message as well. When you don't follow your unique path, not only do *you* suffer, but *anyone that could have ever benefited from your presence suffers too.*

The Power and Responsibility of Your Natural Path

As Fu Yu-Lan said, "Everything is happy if it is allowed to be in accordance with its own nature." When your vocation is aligned with your natural gifts, you become alive. When you can introduce yourself as someone who doesn't just earn a living, but as a man who engages in his purpose, people will instantly feel your vibrant energy. If you have this going for you, who you are and what you are gifted in are one in the same and this integrity is remarkably powerful.

You won't care what others think of you because you will feel no need for approval. The joy you demonstrate in sharing your passions will supersede any desire for people to respect you; the respect will be self-evident. Rather than trying to impress the world with how much "status" you have in society, you simply relax and allow your talents to shine through. Others are *naturally* impressed with how much value you provide and how little you try to take in return.

In order to achieve this level of confidence, you must be aggressive with promoting your core message. You must be able to communicate your value to the world on a consistent basis. The more clarity you possess with who you are, what you value, where your gifts lie, and why your perspective on life is uniquely yours, the more effective your outreach will be. If you feel like you could have done a better job answering the questions from earlier in this chapter, take time to revisit them. Keep working to hone in on exactly what it is that you offer the world and what you stand for. With this knowledge well defined, make sure you get yourself out there! Actively hunt for people you can serve along your Natural Path and create products, services, and media for them to experience to help alleviate their problems or inspire their ambitions.

Do NOT be SHY about sharing your talents. Many of us don't feel worthy of promoting our core message because we mistakenly believe, "I must become hugely successful in what I am doing before I can really promote it. What if someone uncovers my weaknesses and finds out I'm not really as good at this as I say I am?" This is akin to saying, "I really want to lose weight and get into great shape, but I'm worried that if I show up at the gym, people will think I'm fat and will make fun of me. So I'm not going to go to the gym – I'm going to wait until I somehow magically get in shape before I start working out in public."

You have to be BIGGER than your fears. Your desire to HELP others has to be greater than your concerns over people not taking you seriously. Again, you will always find people who will not agree with your core message and may challenge your credibility. So what? They aren't part of your core audience – your message is not meant for them to hear. You need to put at least ten times more focus into who can benefit from what you know instead.

Remember that you have to start somewhere. Promote your message rain or shine as often as you can and don't worry about who shows up. Rather than paying attention to those who point out your weaknesses, pay careful attention to those who point out your strengths. Let the feedback from only those who receive value from you influence how you feel. You'll notice something incredible: they won't care how "little" you know or how "brief" your experience; they will only care about how much you have helped them – and to them, this makes you an immensely powerful person. Not powerful in the sense that you can manipulate or control them, but powerful in the sense that you have EMPOWERED them to lead a more fulfilling life. How could someone walk away from that *not* feeling like you have tremendous credibility?

You have a responsibility to empower as many as you can through honoring your Natural Path. You have a duty to help those who are currently struggling with what previously challenged you and show them how to resolve their problems. You are skilled in specific areas for a reason; you are meant to generously share them. If you hide and play small, never stepping up to offer your unique message to the world, people will never benefit from what you

241

could have taught them. Think about your current role models – those who have inspired you or shared with you their gifts in a way that resonated with you. What if they never accepted the responsibility of following their Natural Paths? What if you never knew they existed? How much would your life be negatively affected?

Don't take this responsibility lightly or assume you will have plenty of time to make it happen. Time is a precious commodity and every second that ticks by with you not giving your gifts to the world is a second you're not going to see again. Stop making excuses for why you're not taking action and become a champion for your cause. Regardless of whether or not you think you are ready for what comes with following this journey, know that you can handle it. You will be loved, you will be hated, you will be lifted up, and you will be vilified. But you will not be ignored. As Theodore Roosevelt said, "Your place shall never be with those cold and timid souls who knew neither victory nor defeat."

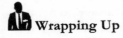 Wrapping Up

I hope I have inspired, pushed, expanded, stretched, informed, taught, coached, and encouraged you throughout these pages. Remember that you have in your possession a reference guide you can come back to whenever you're lacking confidence or feeling doubtful. Far greater than the knowledge in this book, I hope you realize that you have always had the power to shape your life as you see fit. You have the capacity to become the man you have always dreamed about becoming – so let go of the brakes and trust in your vision. My wish is that reading this book has simply helped you believe this fact with more certainty.

I'm going to leave you with this quote, an appropriately anonymous message that sums up much of the contents of this book:

"Someone once told me the definition of hell: the last day you have on Earth, the person you became will meet the person you could have become."

Be the man who shakes hands with the weaker version of you. Own this vision and do whatever it takes to continuously expand and improve who you are. I'll see you on the other side.

NOTES

1. T. George Harris. *The Era of Conscious Choice*. Encyclopedia Britannica Book of the Year, 1973.

2. Nathaniel Branden, *The Six Pillars of Self-Esteem*. (New York: Bantam Books, 1994).

3. Thomas Powell, *You Are the Creator of Your Life*. (Houston: Psycanics, 2003). Quoted from the works of Thomas Michael Powell on psycanic science.

4. David Deida, *The Way of the Superior Man*. (Canada: Sounds True 1997).

5. Sam Keen, *Fire in the Belly: On Being a Man*. (New York: Bantam Books, 1991).

6. Oren Klaff, *Pitch Anything*. (United States: McGraw-Hill, 2011).

7. Sam Keen, *Fire in the Belly: On Being a Man*. (New York: Bantam Books, 1991).

8. Mehrabian and Ferris. "Inference of attitudes from nonverbal communication in two channels." *Journal of Consulting Psychology*, 1967.

9. Amy Cuddy. (2012 October). Amy Cuddy: Your Body Language Shapes Who You Are [Video file]. Retrieved from http://www.ted.com/talks/amy_cuddy_your_body_language_shapes_who_you_are.html.

10. Hemsley & Doob. "The effect of looking behavior on perceptions of a communicator's credibility." Journal of Applied Psychology, 1978.

11. Per knowyourmeme.com: "Hover Hand is an awkward photo pose in which the subject wraps an arm around a companion with their hand hovering away from the companion's body. Often spotted in casual group photographs, hover hands usually signify

that the person feels uncomfortable or lacks the confidence required to make physical contact."

12. Janine Driver, *You Say More Than You Think.* (New York: Three Rivers Press, 2010).

13. For more information, please visit http://cit.cmu.edu.

14. Daniel Goleman, *Social Intelligence.* (New York: Bantam Books, 2006).

15. Michael Ellsberg, The Education of Millionaires. (New York: Penguin Group, 2011).

16. David DeAngelo, *Double Your Dating.* (2001). Ebook file. For more information, be sure to visit http://doubleyourdating.com.

17. T. Harv Eker, *Wealth and Wisdom.* (United States: Peak Potentials, 2005).

18. Viktor Frankl, *Man's Search for Meaning.* (Boston: Beacon Press, 2006).

19. Jerry Bergonzi, *Melodic Structures.* (United States: Advance Music, 1992).

20. Shad Helmstetter, *What to Say When You Talk to Yourself.* (New York: Pocket Books, 1982).

21. Don Miguel Ruiz, *The Four Agreements.* (California: Amber-Allen Publishing, 1997).

22. Mihaly Csikszentmihalyi, *Flow: The Psychology of Optimal Experience.* (New York: HarperCollins, 1990).

23. Antonio Damasio, *Descartes' Error.* (New York: HarperCollins, 1995).

24. Alain de Botton. "On Distraction," *City Journal.* Spring 2010: Print.

25. Mihaly Csikszentmihalyi, *Flow: The Psychology of Optimal Experience.* (New York: HarperCollins, 1990).

26. Eckhart Tolle, *The Power of Now.* (Canada: Namaste Publishing, 2004).

27. Osho, *Beyond the Frontier of the Mind.* (United States: Osho Intl, 1988).

28. Visit http://sedona.com for more information regarding the Sedona Method.

29. Morty Lefkoe's website http://mortylefkoe.com is an outstanding resource for completely eliminating several of your strongest limiting beliefs.

30. Laurence Boldt, *The Tao of Abundance.* (New York: Penguin Publishing, 1999).

ABOUT THE AUTHOR

 Byron "Jetsetter" Van Pelt is a highly successful self-empowerment coach and entrepreneur with a passion for transforming lives. His expertise in personal growth has translated into teaching his clients how to eliminate limiting beliefs en route to creating an irrepressible expectation of success. Through books, video programs, and one-on-one coaching, Byron has helped people all over the world realize their goals in unbelievable ways.

Visit www.byronvanpelt.com for more information.

CPSIA information can be obtained
at www.ICGtesting.com
Printed in the USA
LVHW05222805061 9
620316LV00001B/98/P